HANDBOOK TO ACHIEVE

OPERATIONAL
EXCELLENCE

A Realistic Guide Including
All The Tools Needed

William Boothe
Steven Lindborg

RELIABILITY BILITY®
WEB.COM

Handbook to Achieve Operational Excellence
A Realistic Guide Including All The Tools Needed
By William Boothe and Steven Lindborg
ISBN 978-0-9838741-4-0

Publisher: Terrence O'Hanlon
Cover Design: Christine Rae

For information: Reliabilityweb.com
www.reliabilityweb.com
PO Box 60075, Ft. Myers, FL 33906
Toll Free: 888-575-1245 I Phone: 239-333-2500
E-mail: customerservice@reliabilityweb.com

10 9 8 7 6 5 4 3 2 1

Contents

Acknowledgements

While most of the material in this handbook was originally written by the authors, it has been collected and refined over many years. Some came to us from fellow consultants and even from our clients. We are not always aware of the sources referenced in the articles and papers given to us.

It is our intent to never use another person's material without permission. If that has happened, we ask your forgiveness. Should anyone see material that is theirs, contact us and we will ask permission and give you appropriate recognition in any future publications using that material.

Steve and Bill have written this handbook based on their collective experiences over the past three decades. We gratefully thank these people for all the help, advice and support they gave us:

Dennis Wilkin

Karen Lindborg

Susan Boothe

Mamoun Abulibdeh

Whitney Harris

About the Authors

WILLIAM A. BOOTHE

For many years, Dr. Bill was a consultant working with under-performing organizations to assist them in achieving operational excellence. For several years, he was the president of the largest lighting manufacturing company in the world. Dr. Bill's education includes an A.B in Psychology, an MBA, and two earned Doctorates, one in Organization Behavior and the other in Adult Education. What he has contributed to this handbook is many years of experience "on the firing line." Dr. Bill is now retired and living in Florida.

STEVEN LINDBORG

Steve has over 25 years of experience in manufacturing. He has been a senior manager for several global companies, leading operational excellence initiatives in over 25 facilities worldwide. He has spoken at many management conferences around the world and written articles on the practical application of best practices. Steve has a B.S. in Electrical Engineering and an MBA. He also has CPMM and CMRP certifications. Steve lives with his family in Georgia and is currently working as a consultant.

Preface

Knowing and doing are quite different concepts. Most of us know what to do in our interactions with other people, how to manage and supervise others effectively if our jobs require it, how to raise a family, how to cook healthy, delicious meals, and on and on. At the same time though, we argue with others, lose friendships, manage low productivity, high cost organizations, have kids who are going nuts, taking drugs, dropping out of school and making us feel like failures, and so forth. We're so busy that we don't have time to invest in our kids or to cook healthy meals, so we rely on computers, television and iPods to take care of the kids and the almighty microwave oven and fast foods to keep our bellies satisfied.

Let's take a brief look at this concept as it relates to supervising and managing. Many of us can explain the basics of Abraham Maslow's theory of human motivation[1]. We understand Douglas McGregor's X and Y theory[2]. We can make a chart of Fredrick Herzberg's motivation and hygiene theory[3]. We can discuss the principles of Steven Covey's teachings[4], and so on. We've attended seminars and read books on those and additional management subjects for many years. Our employers sent us to those seminars and, in most cases, paid all the costs. However, in many cases, we see little or no evidence of that knowledge being applied in the workplace.

Why don't we apply what we know or practice what we preach? It's a long road between knowing and doing. The inertia to do what we now know how to do and not rock the boat with change can keep us right where we are. We know we should be changing and adapting new techniques and practices, but the pressure to keep on as we are is formidable. So what can we do about it?

This book is about doing and acknowledges that most readers would say they already know what to do. Why then should you read this book? Maybe you shouldn't waste your time. Though we will briefly review many accepted theories and practices, if you're looking for a new management or behavioral theory, you will be disappointed. If, however, you need to make some changes to your management style and operational practices to improve your productivity, reduce your costs, remain competitive in the marketplace, increase your profitability, decrease your "downtime" and improve employee morale, then this book is for you. You will get step-by-step guides that you can tailor to your particular situation to make these ideas work for you. So you must make a choice to read or not to read. We hope you will join us on this operational excellence journey.

REFERENCES

[1] Maslow, Abraham, "A Theory of Human Motivation", New York Harper ©1943
[2] McGregor, Douglas, "The Human Side of Enterprise", McGraw Hill ©1960
[3] Herzberg, Fredrick, "The Motivation to Work", Wiley ©1959
[4] Covey, Stephen, "7 Habits of Highly Effective People", Simon and Schuster ©1989

"Would you tell me please which way
I ought to go from here?"

"That depends a great deal
on where you want to go," said the cat.

"I don't much care where," said Alice.

"Then it doesn't much matter
which way you go," said the cat.

—*Lewis Caroll, Alice in Wonderland*

*A successful operational excellence program
demands a solid plan and clear direction
or you may be on a trip with Alice.*

Most people don't have to be taught...

...they just have to be reminded.

If you do the things you've always done, you'll get the results you've always gotten.

This is a good reason to learn something new and improve your performance as you embark on this operational excellence program.

Operational Excellence

What is Operational Excellence?

Operational excellence is an enterprise-wide management practice that is "top down" and goal driven with alignment of all efforts at all levels of the enterprise. It stresses management involvement throughout an organization, goal clarity and goal alignment, teamwork, continuous improvement, immediate performance barrier removal, employee empowerment, and, of course, it is customer-focused. Groups and individuals have to change the way they work to achieve operational excellence. Employees will only accept these changes if they can be persuaded to think differently about their jobs. CEOs must alter the mindsets of their employees. This is no easy task. Let's begin your study with the concept of alignment.

What is Alignment?

You're speeding along the interstate on a clear day at seventy miles per hour and all seems right with the world. Your goal is to get home safely and on time. Then, you notice that your right arm is getting tired from holding and applying pressure to the steering wheel to prevent it from turning on its own to the right. When you release the wheel for an instant, your car immediately veers over toward the right lane. To keep your car going straight, you must constantly grip the steering wheel and counter the turn to the right with pressure. What's wrong? In all likelihood, the front wheels of your car are out of alignment. Poor alignment is fatiguing for the driver, causes excess wear on the tires and is downright dangerous, as well as being expensive.

So it is with human organizations. When goals and human effort are aligned, all seems right with the world. Productivity is high, costs are controlled, customer service is excellent, quality is superb, and customers and employees seem quite satisfied. What happens when things change and goals and human effort are not aligned? Stress and strain quickly emerge. Things just don't go right. People seem to be working at cross-purposes, costs creep up, productivity suffers, customer service takes a dive, quality decreases, customer complaints increase, and employees are stressed and dissatisfied. Operational excellence is attained when each and every employee can see the flow of value to the customer and fix that flow before it breaks down.

So, what does it mean to align goals and human effort? Over many years of study and experience, we have identified many variables that must be aligned in order for an organization to optimize its efforts. The variables are:

- Corporate strategy
- Sub-strategies for each division and department
- Organizational culture
- Core technology
- Information technology
- Management process
- Management style
- Work to be accomplished
- Support systems required (for production of goods and services)
- Employee skills, knowledge and willingness to work
- Reward and recognition practices

Human effort in an organization can be considered aligned when:

1. All employees at all levels know what performance is expected of the entire organization.

2. All employees at all levels know what performance is expected of them individually.

3. All employees at all levels are willing to expend energy to achieve both individual and organizational goals.

In reality, what this means is that any member of an organization should be able to tell someone what the goals of the organization are. They should also be able to explain what each goal means to them individually and what they have to do in their position to enable the organization to achieve those goals. Alignment means that everyone in the organization is pulling in the same direction, i.e. sales, manufacturing, purchasing, marketing, distribution, customer service, finance and accounting, human resources, and so on. Only work that adds value is performed. Non-value-added work has no place in an aligned organization. A critical part of alignment is that individuals are willing to work with others in the organization to ensure that the organization meets all of its goals.

Once aligned, the wear and tear on people in the organization is minimized. Productivity, costs, quality and customer service meet expectations, and customers and employees are satisfied. If such practices are adopted on a large scale, the stock market can react favorably. Alignment pays off in many ways.

Change Will Definitely Be Required

The following are some important fundamentals. Change is an inevitable, natural and constant process, not just isolated events. Change requires individuals and organizations to think, act and perform differently. For many, change evokes confusion, fear and resistance. *In order to be successful, organizational change must be led by a strong, informed leader* who understands how to make meaningful changes and help people at all levels in the organization understand and embrace those changes. The CEO and other executives and managers must model the behavior they want from all employees. Then, employees will believe and begin to change.

> *"It's not so much that we're afraid of change, or so in love with the old ways, but it's that place in between fear. It's like Linus when his blanket is in the dryer. There's nothing to hold on to."*
>
> — M. FERGUSON[1]

Steps To Begin The Process

There are some important steps to be followed in order to implement a successful major change: build a shared vision, set clear goals, involve everybody affected, select resources to guide the change process, provide the required training and support, identify and remove barriers promptly, and finally, give recognition and praise often. Each step is explained below in detail.

1. Build a Shared Vision

Leading change can be thought of as a backward process. What this means is that the leader of the change process must visualize and communicate the expected outcome. What will it be like after the change is made? Communicate this to all levels of the organization, clearly stating the intended outcomes of the change required. *Explain why the change is necessary and the urgency for completing the change.* Acknowledge that many may be concerned, but explain that help will be provided for those affected to learn new information and skills required by the change. This is the time for the leader to "sell the change idea" to all members of the organization. Use a variety of media to communicate. Utilize live "town hall" meetings, newsletters, company websites, paycheck inserts, DVDs and other options that may be available.

The better the vision is communicated, the lower the resistance will be later on. Communicate often and with everyone who will be affected. Say it in many ways, say it often, and say it positively and enthusiastically.

2. Set Clear Goals

As a cohesive vision energizes the change process, clear goals — complete with measures and due dates - drive the changes. Later on in this handbook, you will learn the details of goal setting, goal communicating and goal managing. *Setting clear goals is the "heart" of managing the change process, which leads to operational excellence.*

3. Involve Everybody Affected

You must involve members of the top management team and probably many others to develop the vision and the need to change.

Consequently, they will understand the reasons and urgency for making the changes you have identified. Then, you must communicate the vision as stated above and involve as many of those affected as possible in the "how to do it" discussions. Members of the organization will more quickly endorse changes when they have been party to the planning.

The principle here is "involvement produces commitment." When people have a part in the planning process, they typically believe they have a stake in the outcome and are willing to embrace changes as they happen. The involvement also provides a forum for questions and answers, which often helps reduce resistance later.

4. Select Resources to Guide the Change Process

You will need dedicated internal and possibly external resources to bring about the changes you have envisioned. Any change effort will place strain on the organization. As you choose internal human resources, make sure they have the time and talent required. Then, find appropriate outside resources who are experienced and skilled in achieving operational excellence. Build a working team to get the job done.

5. Provide the Required Training and Support

As the change process unfolds, be sure to provide the training required on a timely basis. Change requires people to do things differently. Often they don't know how. People hate to be embarrassed, especially in front of their peers. Sometimes they will resist when they do not know how to perform a new task. Don't let that happen if the embarrassment stems from not knowing how to perform a new task. Provide training promptly and allow time for the employees to become proficient.

6. Identify and Remove Barriers Promptly

Barriers will pop up during the change process. Even excellent planning does not preclude unanticipated barriers. When an employee says something like, "I would if I could, but I can't, because…" you'll know there is a barrier. A process must be put in place to identify and remove barriers so the change process will not be interrupted or unnecessarily prolonged. A process is described later on in this handbook for identifying and removing barriers.

7. Give Recognition and Praise Often

The "Engine of Change" concept, which is fully described in Chapter 4 of this handbook, explains what makes change happen. It consists of goal-setting, barrier identification and removal, and goal accomplishment, followed by appropriate recognition and praise. *Recognition and praise are the fuel for the "Engine of Change."*

Later on in this handbook, you will read detailed instructions about giving recognition and praise. *This is not optional.* The change engine cannot run on an empty fuel tank. Appreciation is one of the most fundamental human needs and it costs nothing except awareness of the need, the accomplishment and the willingness to say "thank you." Executives and all managers must set the example for the behavior they want to see from all employees. We call this "walking the talk."

The balance of this handbook is a series of "mini" case studies of successful change processes that produced operational excellence. The principles and tools described and illustrated will serve you well. Remember, change is going to happen continually. The challenge of management is to foster and manage desirable change.

Here is a quick review of the principles presented so far:

1. Be sure the vision is clear. In other words, can you see what it will be like after the change is made?

2. Set clear goals and measures, and communicate them.

3. Involve as many people as possible.

4. Select experienced and dedicated internal and external resources.

5. Train early and often.

6. Identify and remove things that get in the way (barriers).

7. Give recognition and praise often for progress. Set the example for all employees to clearly see.

In the next part of this chapter, you will read details about the success and/or failure factors of any corporate initiative. A clear understanding of these factors and a willingness to do what this information suggests are critical as your organization undertakes the task of achieving organizational excellence.

Operational Excellence Success Dimensions (The Web)

In this part of the chapter, you will read details about the success and/or failure factors of any corporate initiative. All organizations succeed or fail due to a number of identifiable factors. The diagram below will show you what happens when failure occurs with any factor and the cumulative effects.

THE DEADLY SPIRAL: The spiral depicts the cumulative effect of shortcomings that may be present when incorporating the key success factors in the pursuit of operational excellence. Ten (10) is the highest score and, of course, the scores spiral down to show degrees of success or failure. A score of three (3) or below indicates disaster. All parts of the system must be successful in order for the full implementation of operational excellence to be successful.

The Deadly Spiral

The deadly spiral is a simple construct that can be used to explain many of the reasons behind the success or failure of new corporate initiatives. It logically describes the key success factors of new initiatives and how they interplay to achieve success in new programs. Most importantly, the spiral describes the cumulative effect of shortcomings that may be present in the incorporation of each of the key success factors. That cumulative effect can be seen in the final level of success of the implementation as viewed from the corporate level. We will use plant maintenance as an ongoing example as we explain the deadly spiral, however these principles apply to each and every part of your organization.

Underlying the concept is the idea that implementations are only as good as the least successful of any of the given key success factors and that those shortcomings are cumulative. The web visual can explain why a potentially excellent program fails to deliver the results expected, and ultimately, is abandoned or left to fade into obscurity.

Each of the key success factors will be explained beginning, as it should, with corporate support. The spiral shape is intentional. Each of the key success factors around the spiral is to be considered in a logical series. Each depends on the previous success factor and powerfully influences the succeeding factor as the implementation progresses.

1. Corporate Support

Corporate support includes many ideas and concepts. It wraps the business vision and a set of goals with the resources that will make the vision come alive. Understandably, the resources of money, time and facilities are key to driving the vision to fruition, but this process also includes the visible endorsement by executive management in "walking the talk."

However, the commitment in time by executive management is not to be taken lightly. That commitment must be maintained throughout the implementation. It is the fuel that drives the engine of change. All too often, a well-planned and executed implementation will run out of steam when the executive champion is diverted to other matters.

Conceptually, corporate support is the most fundamental building block of successful change. Without it, implementations will fail, but with full support, the most difficult implementations will get the results desired.

2. Guiding Principles

To understand what a corporate vision is as it relates to an implementation and its goals, a definition of the principles is necessary. These principles are what flesh out the framework that will support the ultimate business vision. Guiding principles take the business speak of corporate management and translate it into a language of measurable goals, objectives, and ultimately, tasks that can be defined, scheduled, measured and monitored. Through this process, links can be clearly seen in translating individual tasks and objectives to shareholder value. Here is where the alignment is traced across all levels of the enterprise. The creation of guiding principles is carefully explained and illustrated in this handbook.

It begins with a description of a work culture embodied in clear and concise statements of vision and mission. These statements should, through identification of what will be important, define the value systems that are to be established. They are articulations of the rallying points for when the organization is under stress. They should reflect the corporate vision in a way that can empower every employee to make decisions that will support that vision.

Guiding principles also encompass the following areas:

RESOURCE ALLOCATION   As part of the guiding principles, a statement of how and what resources are to be engaged and leveraged is necessary. Certainly, the implementation team must be identified, but all executives, managers and the implementation team need to understand where the resources will come from and how they will be organized and focused. *Here is where expressions of corporate support are truly measured and assessed.* Corporate support is easily measured by how well resources are provided, as needed, to facilitate change. A grand idea perceived devoid of adequate resources will fail before it begins.

TECHNOLOGY ENABLERS   In today's business environment, technology is ubiquitous and with good reason. It drives productivity beyond the confines of individual effort and multiplies the combined affect of individual contributions to levels necessary to achieve great results at a reasonable (and competitive) cost. *How technology will be used in the organization to achieve measurable business goals must be defined*, whether it is in the business process itself or in the supporting functions. Often, it is a technological breakthrough that becomes the driving force for a change that either gives a business enterprise its life in a marketplace or ends it.

INFORMATION TECHNOLOGY Business runs on information, whether it's in the boardroom or on the shop floor. Information streams carry the data needed to monitor how processes are working, identify where resources are to be deployed and measure the performance of an organization. *What information technology is to be used and how it will be used must be included in the set of guiding principles.*

WORK MANAGEMENT In the world of maintenance, one of the best examples of defining how work is to be managed is the paradigm of proactive vs. reactive maintenance. Both approaches have the same goal of maintaining a business' assets but do so from very different perspectives. *Similarly, guiding principles should identify the approach a business desires to take since work management streams are integral to the core processes.*

3. Processes

The next step on the implementation spiral refers to the basic business process, which is the heart of value creation. Again, using maintenance as an example, this concept applies to the work processes of task identification, planning, scheduling, execution and closure, all of which make up the business of maintenance. It also includes warehousing, maintenance, repair and operations (MRO) management, the safety/quality/environmental considerations associated with maintenance work, and the use of inspections and testing, such as in reliability centered maintenance (RCM) programs.

These processes should be designed as outlined in the guiding principles. *Resources are inputs to the business process that, when manipulated correctly, result in outputs that have value to customers, internal or external.* Process identification should include the necessary metrics that will monitor the success of the processes in meeting business objectives.

Clearly, if the guiding principles are not sufficient in detail or are short of the mark in some way, the design of processes will be affected. Hence, weaknesses in the guiding principles will be magnified in the design of the processes, which are intended to execute the vision. *Faulty processes are like inherent design flaws that will be revealed much later when correction will be significantly more expensive.* For example, if one of the guiding principles is that working capital will be kept to a minimum, the process of maintenance, as it relates to availability, could be affected. If working capital is expected to be at a minimum, the area set aside for MRO spares may be designed to be less than adequate to support the availability targets for the equipment it services.

4. Structure/Organization

In general, organization follows from process. When processes are formed to fit organization, inefficiencies usually result. Processes will define the requisite organization by identifying the important inputs from people that ensure the process is operating correctly for the desired results. For example, area maintenance may be a good choice in the construction and testing phase of a new plant, but a functional maintenance organization is often the more efficient organization in an ongoing operation.

Another example is the function of engineering, either as design engineering or maintenance engineering. It may be equally effective as part of the maintenance organization or in a separate department. However, in a critical process that operates on a 24/7 shift schedule, integrating an engineering role into a shift may be a better option.

Defining an organization must include the identification of the various roles and responsibilities of the organization members. The organization exists to support the process, not the other way around. Where that support is needed, the people who are assigned to the process must have a clear understanding of their individual roles and the roles of the organization. Responsibilities are needed to distribute accountability so when areas of improvement are necessary, the individuals most involved can be counted on to act appropriately.

Beyond accountability, the relationships between functions need to be clarified. For example, the relationship between maintenance and production should be spelled out so the many facets of that relationship in supporting plant operation are clear to both parts of the organization. Defining who is responsible for daily equipment checks and how the information is gathered and disseminated are important components to both functions. If this is not well defined in the organization matrix of responsibilities, duplicate work, or worse, gaps in the maintenance program could result.

Once the relationships are worked out and the organizational boundaries defined, the communication paths should be clarified. *One way to do so is with a meeting matrix that specifies the intent, frequency and participation of the various meetings to communicate key process information.* With these platforms defined, problems can be elucidated and corrective actions put into place with assigned responsibilities and due dates.

5. Tools

On the implementation spiral, the next step is the identification and acquisition of the tools necessary to maintain the processes. Once the organization has roles and responsibilities defined, the individuals in the organization must have the tools to do their jobs. *Those tools include the myriad of technology enablers, procedures and policies, databases and software packages.* In maintenance, those may include specific computerized maintenance management systems (CMMSs) best suited for the business processes they will support. Other important tools are standard operating procedures (SOPs), checklists and libraries of preventive and corrective maintenance routines.

The tool set should also include the software, firmware and hardware necessary to identify and execute the inspection routines. These may include tools to perform failure mode and effects analysis, set warehouse stocking strategies and perform predictive maintenance tasks. Vibration analysis equipment, thermographic data collection, oil analysis and ultrasonic testing are examples of some of these tools. Others may be local tools to assess equipment condition or monitor and track reliability data trends on critical equipment.

Clearly, the need for a comprehensive set of guiding principles with supporting organizational structure and specific roles and responsibilities form the backdrop that will drive the choice of tools.

Choosing the wrong CMMS, for example, could result in a mismatch that keeps a maintenance organization from meeting its goals.

6. Training

Guiding principles should also identify the importance of training throughout the organization, such as what that training should be and how the developed skills will be maintained. *Here is where the importance of corporate commitment to the workforce is best seen in developing and maintaining the enterprise's human capital. Training, particularly ongoing training, is a clearly visible indication of the level of corporate commitment.*

Part of training is the recognition of the value of group learning. For example, in maintenance, short interval controls are one way to engage a larger number of employees in discerning underlying process changes that provide opportunities for learning across functional lines.

Whereas the guiding principles define the general parameters of training and the importance of training for the business, this step of the implementation spiral supplies the detail on the what, when and why of training for all members of the business. *Training includes reinforcing the technical and managerial skills of the various members of the organization.* Whether on the shop floor or in the offices, employees must know their individual responsibilities to the business. *They must be trained on the use of the various tools provided to them, and they must understand their contributions to the business goals.*

In maintenance, and in fact, all parts of the organization, one aspect of training that is often overlooked is the translation of business metrics into specific tasks. Those in maintenance are generally very good in understanding what it takes to install and maintain equipment, but selling maintenance strategies to senior management is not something taught in school curricula. Being able to translate maintenance recommendations into a business case is a skill that should be emphasized as part of a general training program.

7. Measurement Systems

There is an old adage that says that to control a process, you have to be able to measure it. Understanding how a process is working and if it is giving the results you require and, perhaps more importantly, where to make the necessary changes to get back on track, is a subject of extensive study. In maintenance, those measurements are referred to as key performance indicators (KPIs). There are generally four classifications of KPIs important to maintenance. They are plant performance, process performance, equipment performance and employee performance.

- Plant performance indicators cover a wide range of measures that include overall equipment efficiency (comprised of quality, rate and availability), cost, performance to budget, production, earnings before interest, taxes, depreciation and amortization (EBITDA), return on investment (ROI) and other business measures. They would also include environmental performance, safety, shipping rates, inventory and many other measurable areas.

- Process performance indicators in maintenance may include work order backlogs, aging curves, preventive maintenance completion rates, schedule completion rates, rework, overtime, turnover, as well as availabilities.

- Equipment performance measures or KPIs may include critical equipment reliability statistics, annual cost per asset, inspection results, vibration levels, temperature, and several other operating characteristics that are used in combination to determine overall equipment condition.

- Employee KPIs could include training time, skills progression, turnover, aging profiles, individual productivity, or many others.

Key performance indicators are the process measures that provide information on process performance and are used to monitor and control the process. Looking back, it is obvious that an improperly designed process combined with ill-chosen KPIs could lead to process performance well off the intended or expected results.

Performance measures must be chosen carefully. They must meet some basic criteria to be effective measures. That is, they must provide the performance information intended. They must be measurable, repeatable and controllable. Ideally, someone in the organization would be responsible for this part of the process and would be held accountable for its quality.

8. Continuous Improvement

The last stop on the implementation spiral is the feedback portion that verifies the process is working to expectation, that changes made are monitored for the expected results and that the process can be improved over time. *This is the step that enables the process to be sustainable as people, technology and tools change in the business dynamic.* Here lies the key to making the maintenance process or any process function to expectation. Without feedback, processes will inevitably move away from what they were supposed to accomplish.

The concept of continuous improvement is much like the concept of proactive maintenance. It is a mindset that is fundamentally different from what came before. Where maintenance was once a "fix it when it breaks" mentality, the proactive approach recognizes that better results could be achieved if the maintenance department knows the condition of the equipment well enough that corrective maintenance becomes a logical conclusion to a structured inspection program. *Those better results come in the form of significant cost improvements, improved equipment reliability and availability, and an improved working environment for the technicians and mechanics in the plant.* With a continuous improvement mentality, maintenance managers become asset managers striving to maximize the utility of the plant's assets at ever-lower cost rather than managers tasked to maintain the status quo.

There are a number of tools in the continuous improvement arsenal. Some of the business tools are the periodic management reviews that are done to examine specific key performance indicators (KPI's) related to plant performance. *These reviews look at cost against budget performance, production results against sales projections and other measures of plant performance.* From these reviews come action items that are intended to improve performance.

In maintenance, we could start with failure modes and effects analysis (FMEA) that identify potential failures and develop inspection routines or spare parts stocking strategies to mitigate the frequency and/or impact of failures. Root cause failure analysis (RCFA) is used to identify the causes of failure with the intent of eliminating the causes of frequent failures, or at least reducing their frequency. After action reviews of shutdown work activities are often used to improve shutdown performance that will inevitably improve equipment performance.

Over time, technology, tools and people change and that change provides opportunities for system and equipment performance. With a viable continuous improvement process, the constant change we see in business processes can be the energy that drives a steady improvement in overall process performance.

In the deadly spiral, this last stop is often the downfall of a faithfully designed and executed business process implementation. Without timely and accurate information on process performance, systems in place to use those KPIs as levers of improvement, and clear responsibilities and actions to put improvement efforts into action, any implementation will fall short of what is possible.

The deadly spiral has been framed in the context of an implementation of a new business process. However, it has value in just about any business process improvement effort, including maintenance. When moving from a reactive to proactive maintenance process, the spiral is helpful in reminding us what the important elements are to get the results we seek. It highlights the importance of all of the elements that work together synergistically to achieve great results. It also is a roadmap for systematically laying out the steps needed for a successful implementation.

Without recognizing the critical value of each stop on the spiral, shortcomings in any of the elements are cumulative. An implementation that starts out with the promise of excellent returns will suffer from these combined shortcomings and ultimately fail to deliver. From the perspective of senior management, the poor end results are often viewed as a faulty conception when, in reality, the results are the manifestations of weaknesses in any or all of the spokes on the deadly spiral.

A FORMULA FOR SUCCESS

- Understand your business
- Set goals that require improvement
- Determine measurements (metrics)
- Track results
- Understand results
- Remove barriers
- Be proactive (to prevent problems)
- Solve problems as they occur
- Reward positive performance

WHAT TO DO NOW

1. To the CEO: Now that you have read Chapter 1, you may have enough information to decide if this project is for you. Before you make a decision to proceed, we suggest you read the entire handbook. This way, you'll have an excellent idea of what will be required of you and all the members of your organization. The payoff is obvious from the various testimonies included. The price in dollars is minimal; the price in time and effort can be substantial. After you read the handbook, give a lot of thought to your new knowledge, and then make the decision to proceed or not. We hope you decide to proceed with operational excellence.

2. If you decide to proceed, we suggest you ask all your executives and managers to read the entire handbook.

3. Next, call a meeting of your executives and managers. Tell them what you have decided to do. Review the information included in Chapter 1. Ask for their opinions and support.

4. You may want to choose a person to help coordinate the various meetings and assignments, and assist you with any follow-ups that may be required.

5. When you are ready to continue, assign the reading of Chapter 2 and follow the "What To Do Now" suggestions at the end of the chapter.

●●◉ COMMITMENT CHECK 1

❶ I agree to read the entire handbook so I can make an informed decision about proceeding with the project.

❷ If I decide to proceed, I will begin by following all of the suggestions in the "What To Do Now" section above.

REFERENCES

[1]Boothe, William A., "Managing Change and Aligning Human Performance," A Highland Group Publication, The Highland Group, St. Michaels, MD.

Values, Mission, Vision   2

Values, Mission and Vision Statements

Do you really need these statements for your enterprise? There is much written on these three subjects. We will review the basics, provide some samples, and then refer you to other sources if you have work to do in these areas. First, let's define the terms.

Values

According to the publication *InformIt*, "Values are the core beliefs and principles that govern the behavior and characterize the essence of the organization.[1]" One to seven statements should be established. These may be one-word statements or brief statements of several words. Following are some samples from leading companies. Compare and contrast as you read. You may get some ideas for your own values statements.

Sample Values Statements

1. "We are committed to the delivery of innovative, proven solutions that enable our customers to achieve their potential and/or business in new and exciting ways." (Microsoft)

2. "**Our customers:** We are driven by our customers' needs. We understand the needs of our customers and deliver innovative products and services to meet those needs."

Our people: We respect each other. We work together as one BellSouth Team. This team reflects the diversity of the communities we serve.

Our communities: Everywhere we do business we strive to make our communities a better place to live, work, and grow." (BellSouth)

3. "Cooperation.
   Integrity.
   Lifelong learning.
   Continuous improvement.
   Respect.
   Personal accountability.
   Creating appreciative customers." (Bentley Networks)

4. "Customers.
   Innovation.
   People.
   Commitment." (JCA Software)

5. "Honesty.
   Integrity.
   Excellence.
   Trust." (Unocal-76)

6. "**Service:** To deliver outstanding and continuing service to our customers.

   Commitment: To achieve strong, sustainable results.

   Continuous improvement: To continuously improve our performance, our products and our services.

   Long-term outlook: To evaluate each endeavor and its impact on our long-term outlook.

   Teamwork: To communicate openly and work as a unified team to attain common goals." (Del Monte Foods)

Once you are satisfied with your values statements, they must be communicated to all members of the organization. Should you need additional assistance on this subject, there are many useful sources available on the Web. We especially recommend "Building Your Company's Vision" – Harvard Business Review, 65 1 October 1996.

Mission

The mission statement should be a *clear and succinct representation of the purpose for existence*. It should incorporate socially meaningful and measurable criteria addressing concepts, such as the moral/ethical position of the organization and expectations of growth and profitability. The intent of the mission statement should be the first consideration for any employee who is evaluating a strategic decision. The statement can range from a very simple to a very complex set of ideas.

Sample Mission Statements

"To solve unsolved problems innovatively." (3M)

"To give unlimited opportunity to women." (MaryKay Cosmetics)

"To preserve and improve human life." (Merck)

"To give ordinary folks the chance to buy the same thing as rich people." (WalMart)

"To make people happy." (Walt Disney)

Many believe that the mission statement should be a grand one that is socially meaningful and measurable. The following are some examples of historical mission statements that were truly grand in scale:

Ford Motor Company (early 1900s)
"Ford will democratize the automobile."

Sony (Early 1950s)
"Become the company most known for changing the worldwide poor quality image of Japanese products."

Boeing (1950)
"Become the dominant player in commercial aircraft and bring the world into the jet age."

Wal-Mart (1990)
"Become a $125 billion company by the year 2000."

So, when you are preparing your mission statement, remember to make it clear and succinct, incorporating socially meaningful and measurable criteria, and consider approaching it from a grand scale.

As you create your mission statement, consider including some or all of the following concepts:

- ► The moral/ethical position of the enterprise
- ► The desired public image
- ► The key strategic influence for the business
- ► A description of the target market
- ► A description of the products/services
- ► The geographic domain
- ► Expectations of growth and profitability.

The above information is excerpted from an article "Mission Statement" 1994 by Business Resource Software, Austin, Texas. Should you need more information on writing a mission statement, you will find an abundance of information on the Internet.

Vision

Successful habits of visionary companies have outperformed the general stock market by a factor of 12 since 1925. (Collins and Porras). Vision provides guidance about which core practices to preserve and builds an image of the future towards which the business can progress. In brief, a vision statement should include such things as:

What we *want to be*

What we *want to achieve*

What we *want our future to look like.*

Organizations that know where they are going will simply get there faster. Vision defines the enduring character of an organization, a consistent identity that transcends product or market lifecycles, technological breakthroughs, management fads and individual leaders. It holds an organization together as it grows, diversifies, expands globally and develops workplace diversity. To attain the vision will require significant change and progress. A well-developed vision will guide the way and is part of the vital foundation for achieving operational excellence.

Sample Vision Statements

"Understands that people and systems in the organization must be constantly tuned to customer needs and to management's evolving concept of service excellence."

"The classroom is one in which the potential for learning is open and free to every student."

"To be a leading organization to provide training, knowledge and service all over the world in the environmental sanitation industry."

"Using events to change the lives and minds of people and to bring the talent of people (Africans) and their culture to bear in the global world."

The poster on the following page shows how one company communicates mission, vision and values to its employees.

A special note: Should you determine that you need assistance with developing and writing your values, mission and vision statements, go to the Internet. You will quickly find the resources you require. When this task is completed, you will be ready to move on to the subject of goals.

The Mission, Vision, & Values of Educational Testing Service

 Mission

Our mission is to help advance quality and equity in education by providing fair and valid assessments, research, and related services. Our products and services measure knowledge and skills, promote learning and performance, and support education and professional development for all people worldwide.

 Vision

ETS will be recognized as the global leader in providing fair and valid assessments, research, and related products and services to help:

- **Individuals** make successful educational and career transitions throughout their lives.
- **Parents** understand and use assessments and related products to help their children reach their full potential.
- **Teachers** improve their practice through assessment and professional development.
- **Educational institutions** make informed decisions concerning admissions, awards, and placement; facilitate teaching and learning; and provide useful information to the public on the quality of programs and services.

- **Businesses** use assessment products and services to aid successful performance in the global workplace.
- **Governments, countries, states, and school districts** create equal access to quality education, and develop and use assessments and related products and services fully and appropriately.
- **Measurement specialists** develop fair, valid, and technologically innovative assessments.
- **Researchers** advance the field of educational measurement and contribute to policy debates about critical educational issues.

 Values

ETS is guided by a core set of values and commitments to our employees and to the clients, institutions, and learners we serve, as well as the public at large. Our values are:

- **Commitment to integrity** in all that we do.
- **High professional standards in testing and research.**
- **Fairness and validity in all our tests.**
- **Support for fair and equal access to educational and career opportunities** for all, regardless of social or economic circumstances.
- **Commitment to education reform** through our products and services, scholarly research, and public leadership.

- **Outstanding customer service** that meets or exceeds the expectations of our clients.
- **Recognition, respect, and support for employees** as our most valuable asset.
- **Social responsibility and concern for our neighbors, constituents, and society.**
- **Accountability, openness, and responsiveness** in all we do.
- **Fiscal responsibility** to ensure we can continue to serve our mission for years to come.

MISSION, VISION, & VALUES Created by Educational Testing Services (ETS), Princeton, NJ. Posted in all compay facilities to be seen and read by all employees and visitors. ©2004

Values, Mission, Vision and Goals Pyramid

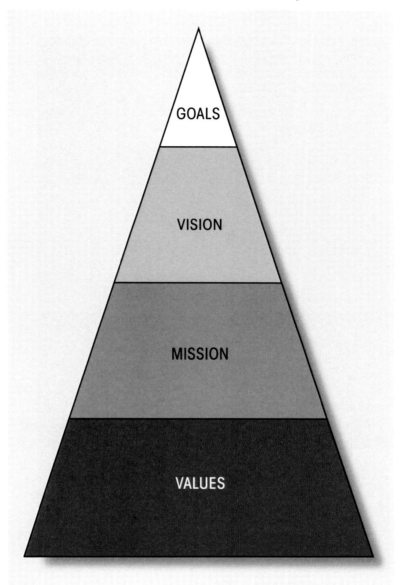

This Graphic Represents A Hierarchy For Creating Organizational Values, Mission, Vision And Goal Statements. Values Are The Foundation. Other Statements Are Created In The Order Shown Proceeding From Values To Goals.

WHAT TO DO NOW

1. Call a meeting of all your executives and senior managers. Advise them that you are asking them to help you examine your values, mission and vision. Ask them to come prepared with ideas for consideration.

2. Should any of you need resources as you prepare for the meeting, there are many helpful resources available on the internet.

3. At the meeting, discuss the information included in this handbook. Cover one subject at a time. Make any changes, deletions, or additions until you arrive at a conclusion for all three subjects and reach a consensus.

4. Develop a plan for communicating your work. Ask for a couple of volunteers to make the communication happen. Be sure to set a due date.

●●● COMMITMENT CHECK 2

① Will you take the actions necessary to make this work happen on your values, mission and vision? This is a task for the CEO.

② Do you realize the importance of these statements?

③ Are you willing to lead this process? (This task should not be delegated.)

REFERENCES

[1] InformIt Network – A Management Reference Guide. An on-line family of publishers known as The Pearson Technology Group, a division of Pearson Education. Hosted by Rich Schiesser, July 9, 2004.

Setting Top Level Goals 3

We've made the case so far that any successful operational excellence initiative must be led and coached by senior management. Usually, that will be the CEO. In their white paper, "The Goal of Management," Robert Rogers and John Hunter reported the following from a 1991 comprehensive review of 30 years of research on the impact of management by objectives:

> "Companies whose CEOs demonstrated high commitment to MBO showed, on average, a 56% gain in productivity." Companies with CEOs who showed low commitment only saw a 6% gain in productivity.[1]"

This most important task cannot be delegated because it is a way of life. Just as one cannot delegate his or her breathing needs, one cannot delegate the life force of the enterprise. There is nothing more important.

> **When a ship misses the harbor,**
> **rarely is it the fault of the harbor.**

We believe the harbor is the leadership and guidance of senior management. Of course, the ship is all the members of the enterprise. So where does senior management begin to establish and communicate a safe harbor for the enterprise? The first and probably most critical step is establishing top level goals. These goals will be rolled down to all levels of the enterprise in language that all associates can understand. These goals will drive the performance of all associates. One consulting firm, The Highland Group, refers to these goals as "driver goals" since they enable the enterprise to continually reach the harbor safely.[2]

What Goals Must be Set?

So, the first question: What goals must be set? Let's review a little history about the evolution of goals, also referred to as objectives.

A review of management and behavioral science literature reveals a common theme about goal setting and goal management as an important management practice. The concept of "task clarity" is often stated as the most important ingredient for human motivation. Most writers emphasize the need to provide clear direction and leadership, and the importance of delegation and accountability are often described. However, the concepts of goal setting by top management, translating and cascading the goals throughout the enterprise, and developing a dynamic goal management system are often absent from the literature.

This is not to say that managers have not been aware of or have not used the practice of goal setting. Surely, goal setting and attainment are centuries old practices. Military, government, business and industrial leaders have engaged in goal setting as a standard practice throughout the ages. The point here is that documenting a specific goal setting practice and acknowledging the power of management with enterprise-wide aligned goals has developed slowly over the past several decades.

In his book, *The Practice of Management*, published in 1954, Peter Drucker probably gave birth to modern attention to goals, which he called objectives. He said, "Objectives are needed in every area where performance and results directly and vitally affect survival and prosperity of the business [...] they spell out what results the business must aim at and what is needed to work effectively toward these results" (Drucker 63)[3]. He also discussed the concept of measurement. "Productivity measurement is the only yardstick that can actually gauge the competence of management and allow comparison of different units within the enterprise and of different enterprises" (71). One additional quote is noteworthy: "Objectives in the key areas are the 'instrument panel' necessary to pilot the business. Without them, management flies by the 'seat of the pants' without landmarks to steer by, without maps and without having flown the route before" (87). *No wonder the ship often misses the harbor!*

It is most interesting that more than 50 years ago, Professor Ducker introduced three ideas that are central to the goal management practice included in this handbook. These are: 1) goal or objective setting, 2) measurement of results, and 3) instrument panel or management dashboard.

Drucker's work had a great influence on managers of the day and for many years to follow. The concept and practice of "management by objectives" (MBO) was born and quickly became the "flavor of the month" that lasted for decades. Anybody and everybody got on the MBO bandwagon. Books were written, seminars were widely attended and managers bought it hook, line and sinker. What happened? MBO is not widely practiced today though it was studied and practiced for many years.

A well-known consultant, W. Edwards Deming, advised his audiences and clients to eliminate goals altogether. Deming observed in actual practice how goals and standards limit performance. He taught that people who are capable of more reach their goals and then stop. In other words, employees typically give what is asked for, even when they are capable of more. Obviously, Deming's ideas had a dampening effect on the use of goals. It is important to note that Deming's experience was largely in the automotive industry where Union work rules probably had more impact on work than goals.[4]

Disenchantment about goal setting and MBO programs crept in for a variety of reasons. Some of these reasons are:

1. Not all leaders (some quite influential) agreed that goals were important.

2. Goals were often written and then not referred to until performance appraisal time that could be six months or a year later.

3. Since goals were not typically referred to and adjusted during the year as change occurred, the goals were probably no longer realistic or relevant at the end of the performance period.

4. Goal setting quite often was a "bottom up" process. Managers followed the advice of Drucker and, indeed, goals were set in every area of the enterprise, but most often without communication or

collaboration with other areas. So, many goals were not related to top-level goals.

5. Top-level goals for the new year were sometimes not released by senior management for a month or more into the performance period. This always created severe problems for those who had to roll down goals in their organizations.

The practice of MBO took on many shapes as managers tried to overcome the deficiencies of the practice. Goal setting never went away, it was just there and was and is practiced in a variety of ways. When asked, most managers will express displeasure with their goal setting methodology, even though they continue to do it, because most of them think it is the right thing to do.

Let's look at a few more recent and extremely popular management books and see what is said about goals and goal setting.

> ► Steven Covey, in his book, *The 7 Habits of Highly People*[5] (1989), makes a strong case for clearly stating your expectations of others. However, explicit goal setting for use in the workplace is not discussed in his book. Covey does strongly support goal setting for self-development and self-management. He presents a detailed process for individual goal setting and self-management. These principles can easily be translated into the business world.
> ► In their book, *Built To Last*[6] (1997), Jim Collins and Jerry Porras include a detailed chapter on the subject of goals. This is a must-read for those who believe in the practice of goal setting and management with a clearly defined goal management practice used throughout the enterprise and championed by the CEO.
> ► It is curious that John Kotter, in his book, *Leading Change*[7] (1996), does not include goal setting in his eight-step process for leading change. He makes a clear case for vision, strategy and employee empowerment, all of which are vital to success, but includes no discussion about goal setting or goal management, which we believe are also vital for success.
> ► Support for goal setting is included in Aubrey Daniels's book, *Bringing Out the Best in People*.[8] His concept is that goal

setting is a powerful tool to shape behavior because with goals and performance measurement, managers have what is required to give positive reinforcement. This book is a must-read for managers who want to learn about the real power of goals and positive reinforcement as management tools that really work.

► One further interesting note: In their book, *Reengineering The Corporation*,[9] Michael Hammer and James Champy have little, if anything, to say about the role of goals. Their basic premise is that success comes as the result of process redesign.

Obviously, there are dozens of books and articles that could, and maybe should, be read to do a comprehensive review of the subject of goals. That is not the intent of this handbook. We can conclude, however, that goals are important, performance measurement is important and feedback to all employees is important. When you roll these ideas together into a comprehensive goal management practice, it gives you one of the most powerful management practices for application in any enterprise. What might a set of top level goals look like? Here is one example:

⊠ ETS OPERATIONS TOP LEVEL GOALS FOR 2002

1. Complete the operations restructure by July 31, 2001.

2. Effectively utilize ETS volunteers for major peak periods by June 30, 2002.

3. Improve productivity by 10% by June 30, 2002.

4. Set and meet quarterly goals to achieve quality improvement in the core processes of registration, test administration and test scoring.

5. Set additional continuous improvement in the core processes of registration, test administration and test scoring.

6. Implement the Operations System for Managing by September 30, 2001.

7. Identify candidates for the succession planning and development process by November 10, 2001.

8. Recognize, respect and support all employees as our most valuable asset at all times.

Goal Setting Considerations

Top level goals must be set while considering many variables, which can help achieve or even defeat success. The following are fairly representative and were introduced in Chapter 1. The variables for your enterprise may be similar.

1. **Corporate strategies:** Obviously, all goals must be aligned with corporate strategy.

2. **Sub-strategies for each division and department:** This allows all lower level goals to be aligned with top level goals and prevent wasted time setting goals at any level that will not be relevant.

3. **Organizational culture:** This is the passion for growth and profitability, for example, present among the management and all employees. You must be careful that your culture will support the goals you set.

4. **Core technology:** Do you possess or can you quickly modify your core technology to support the achievement of your top level goals?

5. **Information technology:** Be careful to not overstress your system. You will want to be aggressive with your top level goals, but also you must be realistic. This is one variable that you may not be able to change in the near term, so look carefully at your present capability and make the best judgment you can about the support you can expect.

6. **Management process:** How capable is your management process to serve you as you manage this highly participative operational excellence? Will it work?

7. **Management style:** A "democratic" style will be required. Employee involvement is central to achieving operational excellence. You must assess this variable carefully to be as sure as you can that your managers can and will support the top level goals and operational excellence requirements.

8. **Work to be accomplished:** You and your management team must carefully collaborate so that the work that needs to be done is represented in your top level goals, and any extraneous (non-value added) work is not permitted.

9. **Support systems required:** Maintenance, shipping and receiving, quality assurance, human resources, and training and development are examples of systems to support success.

10. **Employees' knowledge and skill:** Do you have it, can you acquire it, or can you train the workforce in time to get the job done?

11. **Reward and recognition practices:** This is one of the three cornerstones for achieving operational excellence. Extensive information will be provided later on in this handbook.

There may well be additional variables you must consider. Here is the key point: *You must carefully consider these and other variables you might think of and all variables must be aligned with your top management goals.* We will provide you with the process and much more about goal alignment as well.

POWER PUNCH 2

IT WORKS LIKE THIS...

EXPECTATIONS

- Achieve goal consensus at top
- Create organization-wide linkage
- Align goals throughout organization
- Establish measures and tracking system

CAPABILITIES

- Eliminate unnecessary work
- Identify and remove barriers
- Define new behaviors
- Train and/or acquire human resources

REWARDS

- Publish goals in all areas
- Link rewards with goal achievement
- Implement recognition program

1. Plan to hold a top level goal setting meeting with your executives and senior managers.

2. Advise those who will attend on what the meeting is about. Ask them to read Chapter 3 of this handbook.

3. Depending on the time of year when you hold your meeting, please observe the following: If it is the fourth quarter of the year, use this opportunity to set top level goals for the next year. If you hold your goal setting session at any other time of the year, set goals for the balance of the current year.

4. At the meeting, review Chapter 3 of this handbook.

5. Set at least one goal for each key area of your business. Your total number of goals should be no greater than eight.

6. Check each of your goals against the variables listed in the chapter to assure that each variable will have a positive effect on reaching the goals.

7. When the goals are completed and you have reached a consensus, ask for a couple of volunteers to document your work and to suggest how, where and when the goals need to be communicated.

●●◉ COMMITMENT CHECK 3

❶ Are you willing to plan and conduct the meeting designed to produce top level goals for your enterprise?

❷ Ask for a couple of volunteers to have appropriate media constructed and to help you pour out the goal news to all employees.

REFERENCES

[1] A study by Robert Rogers of the University of Kentucky and John Hunter of Michigan State University, *Journal of Applied Psychology*, Vol. 76 No. 2, 1991

[2] The Highlands Group, St. Michaels, MD.

[3] Drucker, Peter F., "The Practice of Management", page references (63, 71, 87), Harper and Row, ©1954.

[4] Walton, Mary, "The Deming Management Method", The Putnam Publishing Group, ©1986.

[5] Covey, Stephan R., "7 Habits of Highly Successful People", Free Press a division of Simon and Schuster, Inc., ©1989.

[6] Collins, James C. and Porras, Jerry T., "Built to Last", Harper Collins Publishers, ©1994.

[7] Kotter, John, "Leading Change", Havard Business School Press, ©1996.

[8] Daniels, Aubrey C., "Bringing Out the Best in People", McGraw Hill, Inc., ©1994.

[9] Hammer, Michael and Champy, James, "Reengineering the Corporation", Harper Collins Publisher, ©2001.

The Engine of Change 4

What Does It Mean?

It is trite to say again that change is constant. We have rapidly become a world economy with instant communication, competition that we never imagined, technological breakthroughs in both products and manufacturing techniques, with an educated and informed population that wants everything better, faster and cheaper. Every organization struggles to keep up, much less stay ahead. Many are failing. Some are closing shop, others are merging or being acquired, thus creating another category of change. The big question on our minds is, "How can we possibly manage this complicated, accelerating rate of change?"

This transition to a world economy has, of course, created pressures on managers at all levels in business and industry. Remaining competitive, keeping costs in line, creating new products and services that are unique and competitive, competing with offshore low pay rates and getting employees to understand the magnitude and implications of world competition are concerns for all of us regardless of our place in the organization.

While we do not have ready answers for all of these questions, we do have some answers that will help executives and managers to understand and manage internal change. How does positive change actually happen? How can I manage change on a daily basis? These are constant questions. Achieving operational excellence will undoubtedly call for extensive and rapid change. The graphic that follows depicts the major components of how positive change happens. All managers at all levels in the enterprise must understand and properly execute each and every component.

The "Engine of Change" graphic below is an illustration of how the goal setting cascading and translating process is a comprehensive management tool for bringing about desired change within an organization. Refer to the top left hand corner. You will see the words "Top Goals." This refers to the top level goals set for the enterprise by the top management team. The downward pointing arrows represent the cascading and translating of goals to all levels in the enterprise.

Once goals are translated, all employees set about their work to achieve their goals. They will have successes and they will encounter problems or barriers. "I would if I could but I can't," is the phrase you will hear. Barriers should be removed at the lowest possible level so work can proceed. However, the barrier should be escalated to higher levels of management until it is removed.

Prompt attention to barrier identification and removal is critical to making progress toward goals. (See the separate procedure for "Barrier Identification and Removal.")

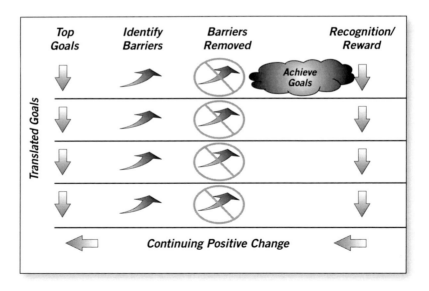

Reward and Recognition

As we stated earlier, *recognition is the fuel for the engine of change.* It is such a simple thing to practice. What can be easier than to say "thank you," or, "I appreciate your hard work," or, "that's really a good job?" In its most basic form, that is what praise and recognition are all about. We often use a triangle to show the relationships of the three critical variables that make up the "Engine of Change."

Recognition

It is intentional that "Recognition" is reflected as the base or foundation of the triangle. And "Recognition" is the base or foundation of the "Engine of Change." Any manager truly interested in aligning the human effort in an enterprise will learn to look for every opportunity to praise good work.

WHAT TO DO NOW

1. This is a short, easy to understand chapter. There is no immediate action required.

2. When you plan your work for Chapter 5, there will be a brief assignment to review this chapter, also.

●●● > COMMITMENT CHECK 4

Are you willing to study this brief chapter until you know it well enough that you can present these concepts to others?

Defining the Organization 5

Structure Based on Functions, Not People

One of the common mistakes and normally overlooked problem is in the design of the organization. We tend to build our structure around people's strengths and friendships. John is a good people person but a poor organizer, so we break some of his roles off and give them to someone else who is a good organizer and so on. Pretty soon, the structure of who does what and why is very blurred. People move, yet roles remain, but no one ever questions why.

The military is a good example of building an organization around functions rather then people. They train people to handle these functions rather than say, "Joe is a poor leader, so let's have him sit back and have Sam take the hill." *The functions that need to take place and how they are best combined into a role is the right way to start.* If you build your group around people and not functions, in time, you will be dysfunctional and need to redesign again. That means you will bring in some consulting firm to tell you to now centralize, or, if you are centralized, to decentralize, and on and on we go.

Whether you are area-based or centralized is not the problem. Either of these structures can work. They all have their good points and bad. The real key is in setting up the structure with the proper roles and responsibilities. What you want to see is that people understand how they contribute and what the expectations are. Then, train towards this, and set up the proper communication process to give feedback. This is really the only way to maintain the continued growth of operational excellence. What happens so often is that we put a great program in place and then the people who helped build it get promoted or move on. If we have not built the structure on functions with clear roles, then the next guy steps up and is lost or changes direction. When this happens over a period of time, you get back to where you started and have to implement all over again.

When you build a roadmap for operational excellence and define all the points, it works as a guide to the next generation. We will include examples of how to do this in the Appendix.

Roles and Responsibilities (R&R)

After deciding the functional organization, strategies and standard operating procedures, the last decisive task to set it all in motion is developing a "Roles and Responsibilities Matrix," with clarity and simplification along with the appropriate level of accountability. Organizations on their quest for excellence may falter due to inadequate, incomplete, or, in some cases, the "self-defining" of roles and responsibilities due to unsustainable initial organizational changes or people turnover.

R&R is just like a musical symphony; one missing action and the whole performance is compromised. Imagine the daily tasks and processes in any organization as an electrical series circuit and the R&R are the connectors or the switches on both ends of any task or process. One missing action and the whole process is compromised or disabled, but in any organization, the gap has to be bridged in order to get the product or service going. In most cases, it will be bridged inefficiently if the problem is resolved outside the clear definition of roles and responsibilities, resulting in a compromised resolution, repetitive problems, inefficiencies and lots of frustration.

Defining roles and responsibilities is a simple, but very efficient, systematic approach in defining who is responsible and who is accountable — in a nut shell, which position performs which tasks. The tasks to be conducted must be defined in a meaningful and definitive way with minimal or no room for misinterpretations or personal perceptions.

Objectives of R&R Definitions

The R&R need to be handled with extreme significance and attention. R&R definitions will be the engine that keeps processes going efficiently. The main objectives of defining R&R should always be aligned with the organization's quest for excellence or, to a lesser degree, operating efficiently. The main objectives can be summarized in the following points:

- ► Functions occupants (resources) will always know what to do and when to do it.
- ► Every step required to complete a task as part of the operations process is clearly defined.
- ► Eliminate process inefficiencies and human frustration caused by task overlap.
- ► Key the document to capture standard operating procedures.
- ► Create an excellent training document for new employees, resulting in less time and resources required to bring new resources up to speed with the organization rhythm.

Why Must We Define R&R?

Organizations often question the need to define R&R. Some may elect to do it anyway as part of a recent change or as a continuous improvement process in mature organizations. Others may not due to a false sense of optimum operation. If you have doubts about the significance of R&R, think about it as an auto engine. Every part in the engine is meant to do a specific task at a specific time, with full coordination (timing) with all other components. If the engine continues running without regular preventive and corrective maintenance, performance will suffer, leading to inefficient and costly operation and, eventually, a complete breakdown. R&R are the initial settings for the engine of your organization and also the routine tasks you have to conduct regularly to make sure you all know exactly what to do and exactly when to do it.

There are signs of organizational inefficiencies caused by vague, unstructured, or self-determined R&R. Let's call them R&R confusion signs. Always look for these signs as part of your operating and performance indicators.

TOP FIVE SIGNS OF R&R CONFUSION

1	2	3	4	5
Repetitive problems keep happening with no specific role being responsible for resolving the problems or the action plan.	Systemic problems or inefficiencies are observed, i.e.: "It has always been like this."	Implicit and explicit accusations of employees not doing "their" jobs are made.	Staff relies on personal relations to acelerate decision making or completion of normal tasks without delays.	Unusually high resource turnover caused by frustration.

R&R Implementation Raci Matrix

RACI Matrix

The RACI Matrix is a simple, practical tool used to document the R&R definition and implementation. RACI stands for Responsible, Accountable, Consulted and Informed. There are three essential components and at least one optional component included in every RACI Matrix. The essential components are the functional roles, tasks and activities, and decisions about who is responsible, accountable, consulted and informed. The non-essential component of RACI Matrix can be a cross-reference field for all related standard operating procedures involved in completing all or some of the tasks constituting a business process. This field can be utilized as a SOP registry. For the purpose of this handbook, the focus will be on the essential components.

R&R Implementation

The R&R definition and implementation exercise must be dealt with as a project with clear time and resources commitments. The major steps involved in setting the R&R in motion are:

1. Gain top management buy-in and full support.
2. Identify all business processes that constitute the core business of the organization.
3. Establish the definitions of responsibility and accountability as the basic components in this project.
4. Utilize the RACI Matrix as a standard tool across the organization.
5. Assign RACI session facilitators.

One of the main pitfalls in identifying the business processes is the lack of clarity and structure when it comes to breaking down a process into logical steps. The following steps can be used as a guideline to avoid such pitfalls:

1. Start with identifying the most critical processes with direct or high impact on the core business.
2. Define the logical sequence of the tasks or activities constituting a business process.
3. Make tasks meaningful and measurable.
4. Start the task with the action required, beginning with a verb representing the action.
5. Define the expected results in every task to avoid having individual perceptions and inherited interpretations replace the consistent definition across the organization. The expected results are usually indicated implicitly by the required action.
6. Maintain visible boundaries between different business processes while listing the tasks.

RACI Definitions

1. **Responsible (R):** The individual who owns the task and is responsible for completing it. It is possible to have more than one individual responsible for the same task if the task is to be completed in different business streams.

2. **Accountable (A):** The individual who answers for the task or the problem, it is where the buck stops. Only one individual should be assigned accountable to each task.

3. **Consulted (C):** Input is required from the "C" individual. Typically, the consulted individuals are the subject matter experts.

4. **Informed (I):** An individual who needs to be informed once the task is completed as a mean of one-way communication.

RACI Matrix Layout

The template may take different shapes or layouts, but the main issue is ensuring it contains the three essential components. The main point is to keep it simple and easy to read and understand.

Business Name: MyBusiness

Plant:

Process Description:

Tasks	Functional Role A	Functional Role B	Functional Role C	Functional Role E	Functional Role F
Task 1	R	A	C	I	
Task 2		I	R	R	A
Task 3	A	R	C	I	
Task 4			R	C	A
Task 5	R	A	C	I	I
Task 6	R				A
Task 7		R	C		A
Task 8	I	R	C	R	A
Task 9	R	A	R	I	
Task 10	R	A	I	R	
Task 11		R		C	A
Task 12	I	C		R	A

RACI Facilitation

The RACI facilitation process is a conclusion of all aspects of roles and responsibilities definition and implementation. This process must be led by a competent person who has strong skills in facilitating cross-functional teams.

The facilitation process can be divided into seven steps:

1. **RACI Concept Education:** Roles and responsibilities concepts may or may not be new to some of the organization resources. An educational session will be very beneficial in accelerating the process by establishing the buy-in at all levels and also streamlining the information needed for a successful RACI.

2. **Process and Tasks Identification:** Identify business processes subject to R&R definitions, starting with critical tasks impacting the core business. The process should go further to break down work into meaningful and manageable tasks or activities. The facilitator needs to engage all functional roles involved in the business processes in order to capture all tasks necessary for completing the process and also establish the logical sequence of the tasks. This part of RACI can be started many possible ways, but the best means is a one-on-one interview with the functional roles involved in the process. The end result of this identification process should be unequivocal logical steps of all tasks involved in completing a business or work process.

3. Plug in all tasks and distribute the RACI Matrix for personnel's individual input. All functional role participants must fill the R, A, C and I for every task on the matrix. The outcome of this step will reveal any R&R confusion. The analysis of the outcome will decide the focus areas and the amount of work involved to bring all resources to an understanding of R&R.

4. Gather all resources involved in the process in a meeting and address every task by asking first who is responsible (R) to complete this task, then who is accountable (A), then who is consulted (C) and lastly, who is informed (I). The results of Step #3 will decide which tasks will need minimal discussion and which will require discussion, debate and agreement. The survey described in Step #3 will reveal which tasks are clear for everybody and which are not. Nevertheless, all tasks must be discussed in these meetings.

5. Analyze and observe the results patterns emerging from the group meetings. The RACI Matrix at this stage is an invaluable tool to evaluate the following components:

   ► Work load balance: Look for balanced "R" assignment.

   ► Tasks accountabilities are assigned to the lowest possible level in the organization where it should reside. Having most of "A" concentrated at a high level in the organization is an indication of wrong conception of accountability.

   ► Look for too much "C," and question the need to consult the marked tasks. Too many "C" tasks may be an indication that training needs to raise the level of competence and skills to streamline processes by reducing the number of personnel involved in completing a task or making a decision.

   ► Look for too much "I," and question the value of informing these roles and what they do with the information once they get it.

6. Compile and distribute the RACI as finalized in the meeting for all participants and the management for final review and approval.

7. Set a date in the future for a routine review for the current RACI Matrices. Such reviews need to be triggered biannually as a routine practice, or when there is a change in process as part of a change in management policy in the organization.

RACI Matrix as an Accountability Indicator

The accountability in all organizations seeking excellence must be considered a key requirement, rather than an objective, for sustainable improvement. Defining and assigning accountability (A) in the process of roles and responsibilities definition is the most influential factor in the success or failure of organizations in achieving their goals, because accountability is the only link between doing the work properly and achieving the intended results. *Accountability is the constant reminder that the objective of doing the work is to achieve the organization's targets and not just to complete the work.*

In general, accountability in a work culture is hard to measure with numbers or KPIs, but it will be evident in the general performance and work atmosphere. The RACI Matrix, when completed, can be utilized as a visual indicator for the accountability level in the organization. As mentioned earlier in the process of RACI, the accountability "A" distribution and where it resides vertically in the organization will decide the fate of the organization's targets. The lower you push the accountability in the organization, the more you empower people, drive ownership, raise the sense of significance and value of your resources, and naturally achieve the organization targets.

RACI Matrix as a Living Document

The RACI Matrix has to be a fundamental component of an organization's management systems and an integral part in the change management system. The matrix review has to be integrated in all change management procedures to guarantee smooth transitions, or adoption of new technology, systems, or changes in general. RACI Matrices need to be reviewed even without the change triggers. There is no optimum frequency for reviewing RACI Matrices, but a biannual sanity review for targeted processes by relevant resources would be beneficial for triggering new or different ideas of doing the tasks of the reviewed processes.

WHAT TO DO NOW

1. As a manager, gather your direct reports.

2. Keep your group tactical and small enough to be very specific in case you have reports that do not interact.

3. Work on the tasks that have some ambiguity.

4. Send your team a draft version first and ask them if you covered all the tasks they question.

5. Let them take a first pass at the RACI Matrix before you get the group together.

6. Allow open and honest dialogue during the review and make sure all involved participate.

7. Make sure that this is a living document and people feel free to come back and challenge decisions made.

8. Be sure to have people cascade this down to their direct reports.

1 Are you willing to look objectively at the functions that need to take place? If not, stop now.

2 Can you look beyond the deficiencies of your employees and train them to accomplish the functions needed? If not, stop now.

3 Can you be objective enough to move people to other seats on the bus or possibly off? If not, stop now.

4 If you are willing to take a tough look at the present situation, then you have a good chance at success.

Process Mapping 6

What is a Process Map?

Most employees will understand their tasks but have little or no understanding of where the work for them is coming from and where it goes after they have completed their tasks. You will probably find that employees in similar or even identical tasks understand and perform their tasks differently. One of the key objectives of operational excellence is to streamline all work and to eliminate non-value-added work.

To facilitate reaching this objective, you must determine the details of every task, where the information comes from that feeds into that task, the details of performing the task and where the completed work will go next. To do this, you must "process map" every task in every department. Following is a small segment of a process map.

Why Process Mapping is Mandatory

Your management has set top level goals. That process is described in Chapter 3. You are now familiar with these goals since they have been communicated to all employees. So what? How will these goals be useful? All top level goals must be "translated and cascaded" down through the entire organization. However, in order to do that you must clearly define roles and responsibilities. You learned about that in Chapter 5, and that work is underway and some probably has been completed. But this is still not the level of detail you will need to set goals at all levels in the organization. Armed with top level goals, organization charts and a matrix of roles and responsibilities, you are now ready to dig deeper and construct a process map for all tasks. **IMPORTANT NOTE:** *The process maps focus on tasks, NOT people. We are charting the workflow, not the people who do the work. After the process maps are complete, you will probably have to make some changes to your employee assignments and your organization chart.*

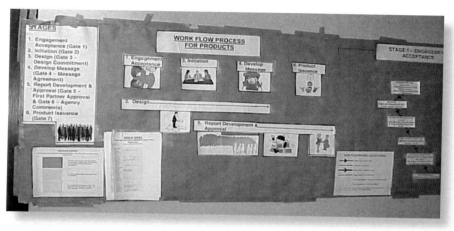

How to Construct a Process Map

Developing process maps will require a lot of time and must involve people who are well informed and can provide the required information and best practices for the process maps.

Steps to follow:

1. Choose a rather simple task as your first one so you will have an early success.

2. Select a team of several people who know this task. Try for no more than six people.

3. Tape a long sheet of brown paper to the wall of the workroom.

4. Ask the members of the team to read this chapter so they know what they are asked to do.

5. Assemble the team for your first meeting.

6. Discuss the process mapping task as described in this chapter.

7. Remind the team that a complete process map shows all of the inputs to the task, all the steps for completing the task and where the outputs of this task go.

8. Begin your work.

9. Brainstorming and other preliminary work can be recorded on cards on a work table so information can be easily changed and saved.

10. After the team has reached agreement, you can now create the process map on the brown paper.

11. Your process map should be starting to look like the sample we showed to you earlier.

When you have completed your process map for this task, invite employees who may have ideas to contribute and ask them to review the process map. Any questions, ideas, or suggested changes should be written on sticky notes and placed in the appropriate location.

When the review is completed and all sticky notes are in place, hold a discussion with the reviewers to gain all you can and make changes, additions, or deletions as appropriate. Now you can draw a complete, easy-to-read process chart for this function.

You also have a vital piece needed before you begin to translate goals, which is the subject of the next chapter.

Continue with this work until all tasks relating to best practices in the enterprise have been process mapped.

WHAT TO DO NOW

- Refer to the "steps to follow" in this chapter and carefully follow each step.

- When you have completed your first process map, use it in a meeting with top executives and managers to demonstrate what your team has accomplished.

- Post your process map on a wall in the meeting room so all in attendance can walk up to it and follow along as you explain the map.

- Hold a discussion and reach agreement on which department or section should be the target for the first set of process maps.

- If no one has been assigned as process map coordinator, make that happen in this meeting.

- Proceed with additional work according to the decisions and guidance of the executive/manager group in the meeting.

●●◗ COMMITMENT CHECK 6

Since this is such a critical step in the operational excellence program, all executives, managers and supervisors must be fully committed. Make sure that happens.

To the process map coordinator: You have a very important job to do with this assignment. It could be a part-time job for you. With each map that is created, you will get wiser on the process. You must demonstrate excellent listening skills and negotiation skills when serious differences of opinion arise. Keep your eye on the target and be the best coach that you can be. If you get in a jam and need some advice, get in touch with one of the authors.

The Goal Setting Process 7

Top Level Goals

Once top level goals have been set for the enterprise, the alignment process can begin. These top level goals will be aligned with the mission, vision and values of the enterprise. All eleven variables listed earlier in Chapter 3 are impacted by top level goals.

After corporate strategy has been determined, the next step is to communicate the strategy through goal setting. In order to not lose focus and defuse the process, we recommend that no more than seven to eight goals be set. These goals can be cascaded and translated for every executive, manager and employee in the enterprise.

The process that will be described communicates strategy by setting specific, measurable goals. Following are top level goals for a division of Educational Tesing Service (ETS), Princeton, NJ, as set by the president and the vice president of the operations division.

The goals for the operations division support the business goals and the mission, vision and values statements. These goals are SMART, that is, they are specific, measurable, attainable, require reach and are time-bound.

Remember, stating goals is only a starting point. Little will be aligned if the goals are not translated and cascaded.

Cascading and Translating Process

First, we will describe the mechanics of the goal cascading and translating process. To "cascade" goals means to begin at the top level and systematically set goals at every level down through the organization. "Translating" is the process of personalizing the goals set at each level so the goals directly relate to the work of the person setting the goals while making sure the goals relate to and support the goals of the next level up. The posting of goals has five steps and is a visual process inviting active involvement of all participants.

Step 1:

Create 4"x6" cards each containing one goal of the leader of the organization for whom goals are being set. Cards for goals four and six from the ETS list look like this:

4. Set and meet quarterly goals to achieve quality improvement in the core processes of registration, test administration and test scoring.	6. Implement the Operations System for Managing by September 30, 2001.

As you can see, these goals are not worded appropriately for the levels in the organization that must perform the work to achieve the goals. Translation is required so these two goals, along with the other six top level goals, will be meaningful to those who must do the work.

Step 2:

Convene a one-day meeting of the top level goal owner and all of his or her direct reports. Ask them to bring all materials relating to goal setting for the current year.

Step 3:

With the top level goal cards posted, use the following example to help explain the translating/cascading process:

INSTRUCTIONS FOR GOAL SETTING MEETING

The vice president of your division has agreed to these goals with your CEO. Our job today is to cascade (or roll down) these goals to your level. Basically, each of you must write (or translate these top level goals) and commit to achieving these goals. When your goals are achieved, this will enable the division to meet its goals. When all divisions meet their goals, the enterprise will meet its goals for the year.

You will write individual goal cards that relate to and support each of your vice president's goals. You will post these goal cards on the wall beneath the top level goal it supports. A card color will be assigned to each person for easy identification as the process develops.

All goals must be stated as SMART goals. SMART means the following:

> S = Specific
> M = Measurable
> A = Achievable
> R = Requires reach or stretch
> T = Time-based

Each card will be reviewed to make sure it meets the SMART criteria. The working process might look like this:

FIGURE 1: Goal cards are color coded according to person and created according to SMART criteria.

When all goal cards are in place, the goal wall will look like this:

FIGURE 2: Once goals cards are created, they are posted on the wall beneath their corresponding top level goals.

Step 4:

After the goal cards for each person are completed and posted, it is time for individual presentations and review. Each person will go to the goal wall to talk through and explain each of his or her goal cards. All team members are invited to listen and ask questions. The vice president (the leader of this team) listens carefully to assure that all "bases are covered." The vice president's basic question is, "If all of these goals are met, will I meet my goals?" Goal cards may have to be edited or added until the vice president is satisfied.

FIGURE 3: The arranged goals are presented by their owners and questions are fielded.

Step 5:

Each of the direct reports to the vice president will repeat the process with all of his or her direct reports. This will continue on down through the organization until SMART goals are set at all levels with all employees. So, that is a description of the mechanics of goal cascading and translating. Participants are typically quite excited when the session is completed.

On the next page are some representative comments made upon conclusion of a session:

"We've set goals for years in our division, but never together like this."

"I found out things about other projects that I never knew."

"Sharing of goals across the division is new for us. I like it."

"For the first time I understand why goal setting is so important."

"We have goal alignment for the first time in this division."

"I'm energized about goals for the first time in years."

"I'll never do one-on-one goal setting again. This is the way to go."

Why are people so excited and pleased with this simple goal process? There are a number of reasons.

1. *It is an open communication process about things that matter.*

2. *The openness and goal sharing of the leader communicates trust.*

3. *The process is active and fun.*

4. *The team learns about its division or department and consequently feels included in the management planning that affects them.*

5. *It is an opportunity to question why certain things are planned.*

6. *It aligns the team and sets it up to be successful during the coming year.*

Let's examine the variables that were listed earlier and see which ones were touched by the goal setting process.

- ▸ **Corporate strategy:** Since the vice president set his goals with the president prior to this goal setting process, the president's understanding of strategy is certainly included.

- ▸ **Sub-strategies for each division or department:** Also included.

- ▸ **Organization culture:** Culture is defined as the distillate of the dominant management styles from inception of the organization until the present time. The culture of this organization supports collaborative effort and values goal setting and alignment. The culture is made manifest in the goal setting process described.

- ► **Core technology:** We can safely assume the organization's core technology will be utilized to achieve the goals.

- ► **Information technology:** Nothing gets done without IT. Make sure your systems can support your goal achievement.

- ► **Management process:** Goal setting is certainly at the front end of the management process.

- ► **Management style:** The style demonstrated by this practice is certainly democratic and collaborative.

- ► **Work to be accomplished:** The groundwork is in place to plan activities, projects, or the work to be done to achieve the stated goals.

- ► **Support systems:** As goal setting, cascading and translating occurs throughout the organization, all support systems will be included.

- ► **Employees' skills, knowledge and motivation:** These are more likely to be engaged in a system that includes all employees in the planning process. The communication and involvement required for goal cascading and translating as described are powerful motivating factors for most all employees.

- ► **Reward and recognition practices:** An important way to provide recognition. All employees are included in the goal setting process that will align their work with others for the coming year. This is an excellent way to recognize employees.

In summary, it is quite easy to see that participative goal cascading and translation touch all of the identified variables that must be aligned in order for an organization to optimize its efforts. The outcome will be aligned value-added goals for each person in the entire organization. The probability of the enterprise meeting its goals is vastly increased, costs will be optimized as all units and employees work together and customer service will be the best in class. What additional arguments are needed to convince organizations to adopt this simple, but profound practice?

Documenting Goals

You have many options for documenting and following up on your goals and the goals of others in your organization. Some organizations create special forms for this need. Others simply type or write the goals as they would any other information. However, to fully utilize your goals and the goals of your organization, it is helpful to have a way to easily document and update the goals, to track and record progress, and to access goals according to the type of goal, employee, due date, and so on. Many programs are available. Once again, go to the internet and assess the offerings. For purposes of illustration, we chose ManagePro*. It is an excellent program and is currently being used by many of our past clients.

We recommend ManagePro, a software program designed as a performance management system. With a small investment in time, you and your team can reach new levels of performance. You can easily record your goals, as well as the translated goals and action plans of your direct reports. As you monitor progress, you can make appropriate notes. You can also attach relevant documents, such as e- mails, memos, reports and the like. You will then have in one convenient place all that you need to conduct comprehensive and meaningful daily, weekly, or monthly reviews with your people. You will be prepared for coaching and to give recognition for progress and completed work.

In summary, ManagePro allows you to:

- ▸ Record SMART goals
- ▸ Cascade and translate goals from top level to all levels
- ▸ Record action plans for achieving goals
- ▸ Identify issues and barriers to achieving goals
- ▸ Access goals in a variety of ways
- ▸ Record results and progress
- ▸ Attach any related information
- ▸ Easily monitor progress
- ▸ Be prepared for feedback and coaching

* *Permission granted by Rodney Brim, President of ManagePro*

- ► Document the coaching session
- ► Recognize employees according to progress toward goals
- ► Be fully prepared for periodic performance appraisals
- ► Delegate goals to others in your organization
- ► Communicate status to selected ManagePro users.

There is a built-in tutorial and an on-screen management advisor to help you on a variety of issues. With ManagePro, you will have a basic organization structure to work from people, goals, action plans, progress notes and to-dos. It is a comprehensive management tool.

A Performance Management System
A Recipe for Success

Most companies compete in an environment that is in a constant state of flux. Goals change, plans change, customers' needs evolve, new technologies enable improved cost and quality, competitors change strategies, and the list goes on and on.

As a result, most companies, in one or more phases of their lifecycle, are faced with the challenge to improve their performance, their efficiency and their effectiveness. They are faced with the challenge to improve upon the way they historically have operated, no matter how successful they were in the past. A number of performance management systems have been designed to help you meet this performance challenge with a simple four-step process.

1. Define where you are going, why and what's expected. (Set clear, robust, defined SMART goals.)

2. Build and work a realistic action plan to achieve the goal (an action plan that takes into account resources and obstacles).

3. Monitor and respond to feedback loops on progress (rapid response to both project and performance feedback).

4. Build and manage a high performance information system (a system to support and connect the above three steps).

Step 1:

The first step in aligning human effort and achieving high performance starts with a clear definition of the goals, objectives, or projects — a robust definition that is based upon customer requirements and directly answers the questions of who, what, when and how much. A definition may include the following:

- ► What is the defined outcome? What specific results are desired?
- ► When must they be delivered?
- ► How will we know if we are successful? What does the customer want?
- ► What skills should your people develop in the process, so that they can meet this objective and even more challenging assignments in the future?

This up-front agreement on goals is especially important if you want to delegate to or empower people effectively. If you delegate without clarity and without grounding in requirements and measurement, you risk being surprised by less-than-satisfactory results.

Step 2:

The second step for high performance, creating a realistic and well-founded action plan, is essential for reaching the goals you and your direct reports have agreed upon. It is the front end of the "plan, do, review" cycle. A good action plan is the last step in translating and cascading a goal. It specifies the tasks and next steps in a "what, who, by when" format and takes into account the issues and obstacles to be encountered, the resources available and the time available.

Goals without a solid action plan are no more effective than New Year's resolutions. They exist as aspirations, but don't provide a realistic framework for people to work by. In fact, without an action plan, most people resort to fighting fires and managing a to-do list as a way to work - definitely not high performance.

BENEFITS: Providing managers with a tool that collects and organizes all of the information and expert advice helps track and manage performance in a way that:

- ► Increases your group's probability of meeting challenging business goals.
- ► Helps you diagnose and resolve complex people management issues.
- ► Helps you create appraisals and skill development plans.
- ► Is based on documented results and behavior.
- ► Develops employee and team capabilities.
- ► Improves employee morale and commitment.
- ► Increases your ability to manage large numbers of people.
- ► Develops your own managerial skills.
- ► Provides a performance audit trail for promotion, compensation and out placement decisions.

Steps 3 and 4 are discussed in detail in upcoming chapters of this handbook.

72 % of performance challenges are caused by unclear or no expectations, or little or no feedback

4

Goals should be "SMART"

S: Specific

M: Measureable

A: Achievable

R: Requires reach

T: Time-based

UN-SMART GOAL

"Reduce scrap"

SMART GOAL

"Reduce scrap from 12% to 5% by June 2011"

Team's individual objectives: To achieve the 5 main objectives, which were broken down to individual objectives and distributed to the team. Here is the list of individual objectives:

Objectives	Responsible
1. Production volumes and costs	All
1. Create structure for outage planning milestones	Allen
2. PS shut down improvement	Allen
3. Capex improvement – schedule monitoring	Allen
4. Support Seattle in PS, development of project managers	Allen
1. Support plants to achieve production volumes and costs	Curt
2. Workforce training	Curt
3. Equipment assessments	Curt
1. Reinstall OPEX at HE, TD and AR	Sal
2. Improvement of PMRs, critical spares and checklists	Sal
3. Improvement of lubrications and vibration systems and programs at HE	Sal
4. Completion of skills assessment and training program at HE	Sal
1. Reinstall OPEX systems	Dennis
2. Implement reliability programs in the plants	Dennis
3. Bill of materials updated/completed for Critical A	Dennis
1. Support Seattle PTS project	Will
2. Survey plant PTS	Will
3. Support implementation of PMs related to PTS	Will
1. Update and complete PMs and BOM for Critical A equipment at 6 main plants	Karen
2. Improve and standardize the plant's planning and scheduling process	Karen
1. Create a reporting system for PMR and BOM and a maintenance board that shows the plant's maintenance performance	Karen
1. Get better knowledge of industry and manufacturing through training	Jed
1. Perform SPA functions CMMS	Jed
1. Re-implement and modify PMs visual inspection sheet procedure and practice	Jed

Individual objectives based on the team's objectives

1. Call a one-day meeting of the CEO and all of his or her direct reports. Tell the planned attendees that you are going to accomplish the first round of goal translation and cascading. Ask attendees to carefully study Chapter 5 of this handbook so they will be prepared to participate. Also request that they bring all goal related documents pertaining to the current year to the meeting.

2. At the beginning of the meeting, review Chapter 4 and Chapter 5 of this handbook to be sure that all attendees understand the goal setting process that will be followed.

3. Before the meeting, prepare 4"x6" cards with one top level goal on each card.

4. Post these cards on a "goal wall" as illustrated in this chapter of the handbook.

5. Read aloud the "Instructions for Goal Setting Meeting" shown in this chapter.

6. Advise attendees that all goals must be SMART.

7. Take time now for each attendee to write goals for themselves that support each top level goal. Post all goal cards on the goal wall beneath each top level goal. See the images in this chapter for guidance.

8. Next, each attendee will go to the goal wall, one at a time, and review his or her goals. The executive who called the meeting will listen carefully, ask questions and make sure there are appropriate, translated SMART goals to support each top level goal and all variables have been considered.

9. Choose a system for documenting your goal translation work.

10. When this work is completed, instruct all attendees to have comparable goal translation meetings with their direct reports and so on down through the organization until all goals are set. Be sure all goals are documented using the performance management system you have chosen.

Operating Information/ Reports

8

Why Operating Reports?

One of a manager's primary responsibilities is to provide the support necessary for the work in the area to be completed. In order to accomplish this task, a manager has to think about and control a number a variables, including company goals (e.g., quality and customer service, cost containment), area goals (e.g., reduction of errors, staying on schedule), and individual and performance goals (e.g., production expectations, workforce development and advancement criteria).

There are different sets of operating reports based on time: daily reports for overseeing the recent actions and results, weekly reports for seeing the truer picture to manage by, and then monthly rollup reports. It is important to understand that you can over-steer the boat by reacting too quickly, but on a weekly basis you can begin to understand trends and if the slight corrections are working. In dealing with the review meeting, it is important to have all the facts first and only review the variances to target. Too often we drown our people with numbers and reports that really only restate the same numbers again and again.

Operating reports tell managers what was actually accomplished against the planned goals and targets. They are after-the-fact score sheets. Reporting documents display actual results, which, in turn, enhance the ability to take corrective action and further forecast and plan. Through the evaluation of past events (performance, attainment, quality indicators) managers can improve their prediction of future resource performance and development requirements.

DAILY WEEKLY OPERATING REPORT

									Week Number	11	
									Week Ending	10-Nov-02	
									Completed by J.	Salaman	

Area	Key Performance Indicators	Unit of Idees	2001 Base	Target/2002 Y/E	Daily Plan		Monday	Tuesday	Wednesday	Thursday	Friday	Saturday	Sunday	Weekly (mtd)
Quarry	Daily Crusher Production	Tons	3245	7072	6560	Daily Plan	6,500	6,500	6,500	6,500	6,500	3,250		35,750
						Actual	4,102	3,245	2,896	4,104	2,301	1,234	0	17,882
	Feeder Run Hours	Hours	6.2	13.6	13.6	Daily Plan	13.6	13.6	13.6	13.6	13.6	6.8		74.8
						Actual	11.8	11.8	10.9	12.9	13.1	5.9		48.7
	Feeder Availability (Uptime)	%	62.4	80.0	80.0	Daily Plan	80.0%	80.0%	80.0%	80.0%	80.0%	80.0%	0.0%	80.0%
						Actual	55.9%	21.3%	67.3%	59.0%	45.6%	67.8%	#DIV/0!	85.3%
	Crusher Rate BDP=520.1	TPH	396	520	480	Daily Plan	460	460	460	460	460	460	480	480
	Crusher O.E.E. (net)	%	47.5	71.4	71.4	Daily Plan	335	365	398	401	348	321	280	367
						Actual	71.4%	71.4%	71.4%	71.4%	71.4%	71.4%	0.0%	71.4%
	Labor Hours Used	Hours		64	64	Daily Plan	36.4%	42.3%	37.7%	53.4%	30.0%	8VALUE!	#DIV/0!	39.1%
						Actual	64	64	64	64	64	64		320
	Overtime	Hours	0	0	Daily Plan	88	59	84	64	70	0	0	325
						Actual	0	0	0	0	8	0	0	10
	Hard Overburden	Tons				Actual	4	0	0	0	0	0	0	0
	In Pit Waste	Tons				Actual	0	0	0	0	0	0	0	0
	Soft Overburden	Tons				Actual	0	0	0	0	0	0	0	0
	Ore	Tons				Actual	0	0	0	0	0	0	0	0
	Waste Haul Tons	TPD				Actual	0	0	0	0	0	0	0	0
	Waste Ratio	%				Actual	0%	0%	0%	0%	0%	0%	0%	0%
Kilns	Daily Production	Tons	1027	1301	1125	Inv. Varianc	0	0	0	0	0	0	0	0%
	Quick Lime- from kiln rate					Inv. Meas.	1,045	1,067	998	1,002	1,023	1,002	1,027	1,027
	Inv. / shipment est.					Calc. Inv.	1,045	1,067	998	1,002	1,023	1,002	1,027	1,027
	Daily Production	Tons	373	494	494	Inv. Varianc	13.6	13.6	13.6	13.6	13.6	6.8		
	Hydrate- from rate					Inv. Meas.	882	995	857	995	374	333	333	333
	Inv. / shipment est.					Calc. Inv.	372	387	298	297	323	323	333	333
	Kiln #2 Rate	TPD	355	491	375	Daily Meas.	1,764	1,289	1,293	1,154	1,267	-19	-149	-149
						Actual	375	375	375	375	375	375	375	2,059
	Kiln #3 Uptime BDP=504 tpd	%	80.2	95.0	95.0	Actual	345	324	333	321	345	298	323	2,289
	Kiln #2 Uptime	%	57.5	92.3	92.3	Actual	78.0%	78.0%	50.0%	79.2%	78.6%	74.6%	63.9%	52.3%
	Kiln #3 Rate	TPD	672	810	750	Daily Meas.	92.3%	92.3%	92.3%	92.3%	92.3%	92.3%	92.3%	92.3%
	Kiln #3 O.E.E. BDP=850 tpd	%	96.3	99.0	99.0	Actual	53.4%	50.1%	33.0%	50.4%	44.1%	53.7%	53.7%	53.9%
						Actual	750	750	750	750	750	750	750	4,560
	Kiln #2 O.E.E.	%	75.5	95.3	95.3	Actual	589	601	643	589	599	612	654	4,266
						Actual	100.0%	64.2%	87.5%	99.2%	91.3%	100.0%	100.0%	612
	Labor Hours Used	Hours	N/A	144.0	144.0	Actual	93.3%	93.3%	93.3%	93.3%	93.3%	93.3%	93.3%	93.3%
	Other Hours	Hours	N/A	28.8	28.8	Actual	38.3%	66.2%	69.7%	64.6%	65.7%	76.9%	64.3%	64.3%
	Fuel Efficiency K-2		N/A			Actual	156	170	144	180	144	190	195	1149
	Fuel Efficiency K-3		N/A			Actual	12	26	0	2	0	46	51	137
	Power Consumption	kwhrs used	N/A			Actual	#DIV/0!	#DIV/0!	#DIV/0!	#DIV/0!	#DIV/0!	#DIV/0!	#DIV/0!	#DIV/0!
		kwhrs / ton	N/A			Actual	65,763	66,083	64,311	64,532	64,321	63,888	72,209	63,917
Hydrators	#1 Atmospheric Production	TPD	124.3	247.0	247.0	Daily Plan	63.98	71.44	65.89	70.91	69.21	70.21	66.05	68.10
						Actual	208	247	247	247	42	247	247	247
	#1 Atmospheric Rate BDP=10.1	TPH	7.7	12.0	12.0	Actual	82	108			8	138	151	496
	#1 Atmospheric Uptime	%	61.8	80.0	80.0	Actual	7.7	6.5			7.8	6.7	7.0	6.9
	#1 Atmospheric O.E.E.	%	40.0	70.0	70.0	Actual	44.2%	69.2%			4.2%	85.6%	89.6%	73%
	#2 Atmospheric Production	TPD	100.0	247.0	247.0	Daily Plan	28.4%	37.5%	0.0%	0.0%	2.7%	47.8%	52.6%	42.2%
						Actual	200	247	247	247	42	247	247	661
	#2 Atmospheric Rate BDP=10.0	TPH	6.3	12.0	12.0	Actual	12.0	12.0	0.0%	0%	0%	#DIV/0!	#DIV/0!	#DIV/0!
	#2 Atmospheric Uptime	%	42.1	91.6	91.6	Actual	0%	0%	0%	0%	0%	0.0%	0.0%	0.0%
	#2 Atmospheric O.E.E.	%	26.7	70.0	70.0	Actual	0.0%	0.0%	0.0%	0.0%	0.0%	0.0%	0.0%	0.0%
	Carson Production	TPD	127.9	247.0	247.0	Daily Plan	241	201	201	201	52			1,166
	Carson Rate BDP=15 TPH	TPH	10.9	14.5	14.5	Actual	14.4	0.0%	0.0%	0.0%				
	Carson Uptime	%	49.0	80.0	80.0	Actual	0.0%	0.0%	0.0%	0.06%	0.0%	0.0%	0.0%	0.0%
	Carson O.E.E.	%	35.8	80.6	80.6	Actual	80.6%	80.6%	80.6%	80.6%	80.6%	80.6%	80.6%	80.6%
Bag Packing														
		Total Tons				Actual	115	36	136		73			
		tph		135	135	Actual	14.4	4.5	17.0	0.0	9.1	17.9	8.4	17%
				15		Actual	48	17.5	17.5	24.0	21.9	24.5	10.6	10.6
	Bag Pack Labor Hours Used	Hours		16	18	Actual	17.5	24.0	17.5	24.0	33.3	24.5	12.3	153.0
	Bag Pack Overtime Hours	Hours			20	Actual	50.5	40.0	1.5	0.0	13.0	24.5	12.3	82.8
	Hydrator Labor Hours Used	Hours		40	40	Actual	40.0	40.0	40.0	61.3	61.3	61.5	59.8	395.8
	Overtime	Hours		8	8	Actual	2.3	1.8	2.3	1.3	0.0	61.5	59.8	181.8

DAILY WEEKLY OPERATING REPORT - This is an example of what an operating report may look like.

This report provides daily and weekly information on the planned versus actual performance in a cement production plant. Production information on Quarry Operations, Kiln Operations, and Hydrator Operations is provided. It shows on a daily and weekly basis areas of excellent production which meets targets and those areas where corrective action may be required.

Operating reports represent a summation of what was planned and the results that were achieved as a result of the plan, and, in some cases, in spite of the plan. The operating report is a management tool that provides a means of setting and managing short-term goals in pursuit of achieving long-term goals.

Importance of an Operating Report

An operating report is the key management tool featured in the review phase of the "plan, do, review" management cycle. The operating report is a "management dashboard" and summarizes what happened. Management action is required to reinforce positive performance, or to change negative performance and, just as importantly, perpetuate the management cycle effectiveness.

Operating reports provide a frequent comparison of a manager's success in matching anticipated work requirements and the human resources necessary to complete the work. There are three primary ratios incorporated in a standard operating report used to facilitate comparisons between resources and work. These ratios are:

1. **% Utilization:** *Compares hours to hours.*
   The percentage is calculated by dividing the hours available to work on earned hours by actual hours at work. A number less than 100% reflects time taken away from routine work for training, special projects, meetings and other non-routine activities (e.g., fire drills, social events). Utilization of 100% would mean that all of the hours available for work were spent on routine area activities. Utilization greater than 100% is impossible.

2. **% Productivity:** *Compares the measured amount of work completed against the hours consumed in completing that work.*
   To ensure proper application and interpretation, the "earned hour" concept is commonplace in all work groups. A productivity rate

greater than 100% would mean that work is being completed above the expected rate of production. (e.g., hours spent in meetings, training and on special projects are not included in this calculation.)

3. **% Attainment:** *Compares planned and actual work output.*
In setting attainment targets, it is important to review best demonstrated performance or BOP. This is a number normally developed by looking at the highest consistent rate over a period of time, say a week or even a month. You then set this as the target for attainment to have a more accurate understanding of possible output. A number greater than 100% means that the work area completed more work than planned. (e.g., measured units of work, such as a telephone inquiry, internet response, completed resolution, production rate, or print run). Attainment of 100% would mean that the value of work planned matched the amount of work completed.

An assessment of area performance is an assessment of one or more of the three ratios.

There are other indicators that are tracked that are specific to the nature and objectives of the diverse work areas within precision manufacturing operations. For example, backlog and aging are critical decision drivers in the choice of whether to bring in contractors or use overtime, but may have no application at all in kiln run time. While quality considerations affect work of all areas, the overall product quality is measured separately to provide a total picture of product performance. Environmental numbers have taken on new importance to manufacturing. The high cost of non-compliance can be so devastating and possibly cause a plant to close. Though they may not make an impact to production, numbers like these need to be seen by all to ensure there is no possibility of violation.

How to Use Operating Reports

Reporting documents can be used to help managers focus attention on maximizing results. For example, you may review the reporting documents from your department (plan to process 500 items a day) and find that over the last four weeks the number of items processed per week has declined (and performance percentages have also declined). This information should give management and supervision an indication that problems are developing in the area.

In designing a system for a particular area or function within an organization, management should determine what information is needed to manage this area or function. Too much information can be just as bad as too little information. The key to an effective reporting system is its usefulness, not its complexity.

Operating reports highlight a number of possible exceptions. Exceptions to planned volumes of work, planned resource hours available, planned work completed and embedded measures (e.g., reasonable expectancies). Any comparison of planned and actual statistics that yields anything more or less than 100% is an invitation to ask the question, "Why?" The manager's role is to support the work group in pursuit of a level plan and actual ratios in all situations in order to meet company, group, area and individual goals.

A common follow-up question on the floor is, "What is preventing us (you, me) from achieving our goal?" The resulting action taken to eliminate these barriers is the true value of effectively using numbers to assist in the management process.

One further note about operating reports: not all job performance can be easily measured on a short term, daily, or weekly basis. Other forms of reporting will have to be developed. Whenever "Key Volume Indicators" (KVIs), "Key Performance Indicators" (KPIs), or "Reasonable Expectancies" (REs) can be established, the operating report shown as an example at the beginning of this chapter can be used.

Some Important Definitions (A Review)

1. **Utilization:** *Compares hours to hours.*
   Percentage of the actual time spent performing a task compared to the expected time to perform the task (standard or reasonable expectation).

2. **% Productivity:** *Compares the measured amount of work completed against the hours consumed in completing that work.*

Some examples are hours spent in meetings, training and on special projects that are not included in this calculation. To ensure proper application and interpretation, the "earned hour" concept is commonplace in all work groups. A productivity rate greater than 100% would mean that work is being completed above the expected rate of production.

3. **Attainment:** *Compares planned and actual work output.*
A number greater than 100% means that the work area completed more work than planned. Attainment of 100% would mean that the value of work planned matched the amount of work completed. An assessment of area performance is an assessment of one or more of the three ratios.

You have just read a short, rather simple operating report and you also read a brief description of its importance and use. This chapter and the next chapter go together. You will have a short assignment here and a more involved assignment after you study Chapter 9.

1. Study the report at the beginning of this chapter and you will find the following key performance indicators in use. We will give you some numbers to calculate to check for understanding:

   a. % Utilization: The crewman works 40 hours per week. He has a 1-hour safety meeting weekly and a half hour paid lunch daily. He has 15 minutes each day to shower. If he works the rest, what is his utilization? *Answer: 88% This is extremely high and uncommon, but it is only an example.*

   b. % Productivity: Two men are scheduled for a 6-hour job, but they get it done in 7 hours. What is their productivity? *Answer: 85%*

   c. % Attainment: The best demonstrated performance is 400 tons per day (TPD), the target is 350 TPD, and the actual is 325 TPD. What is the attainment? *Answer: 81%*

2. Review the sample "Daily Weekly Operating Report" to start getting ideas about the ones you will develop for your organization. Of course, each functional area will require one or more operating reports specifically developed for them.

3. You might want to make a list of those people in your organization who have the appropriate skills to develop these reports. They could make up a task force to accomplish this important work. Also, be aware that the operating reports must be closely related to the roles and responsibility charts you will learn about in Chapter 11.

●●● COMMITMENT CHECK 8

❶ This is a very important part of operational excellence. If you don't measure it, you probably cannot change or fix it. If you don't record information, review it and take appropriate action soon and often, you can be off track and not know where or how much. This information also provides what you need for reward and recognition, which is the fuel that drives all performance.

❷ Make sure you and all of your executives and managers understand and are committed to this process.

Using Information

Monitoring Results

Successful performance management also requires the third step outlined in Chapter 7: implementing the action plan and responding to feedback gained from monitoring interim progress at appropriate intervals. In order to be feedback-responsive, you must monitor progress and respond to changes. Identifying and removing barriers to achieving a goal is a major management task during this "doing" phase of the "plan, do, review" cycle.

Frequent and positive communication with the workers is critical for identifying barriers to achieving goals. When a worker says, "I wish I could, but I can't, because," *the statement following the "because" is likely to be a description of a barrier that needs to be removed.* You may need to solve a process problem, develop a temporary work-around, modify the action plan, change the goals, add or delete staff members, or call in a Six Sigma "green belt" to help solve a problem. But you won't know if you are on or off course until you regularly monitor progress. Responding to feedback also includes the important people feedback loop of *feedback, coaching and recognition of performance.* If performance appraisals, compensation, promotion, job responsibility and other forms of recognition are integrally linked to contribution, each of your direct reports and teams will try that much harder to excel.

One of the most often heard complaints about goal setting processes is that goals are set and then not referred to during the period of performance. Then, at performance appraisal time, goal achievement is used as the basis for the appraisal. Often the goals are out of date due to many changes that were not recorded, so, the appraisal is seen as inadequate and unfair.

A goal management process must be dynamic in order to be successful. In other words, it must be used on an ongoing basis as a management tool. This begins with the progress monitoring process. Depending on the type of business and the functions within the business, goals may be monitored daily. In some cases weekly monitoring, such as the operating report shown in the previous chapter, is appropriate, and, yet, in other situations, monthly monitoring is okay.

The point here is that you have documented what you and your team must accomplish to assure that your manager's goals are met and so on up through the organization to make sure top management goals are met. During the goal setting process, your goals were linked and aligned throughout the enterprise. This gives you the results you and your team must achieve.

Monitoring means that you will use these goals as your guide throughout the performance period. To do so, you have to set up metrics so you can measure your performance. The task now is to watch what is happening. What are the metrics telling you about goal progress? Are you on track, off track, ahead of schedule, behind schedule, over costs, under costs, and the like according to the metrics you have developed?

High performance requires managing and making the information to connect the first three steps accessible to the executive/manager and their team. We call it leveraging information, and are referring to the process of storing, retrieving and getting multiple uses out of information so that its value increases exponentially.

Careful documentation, along with your metrics and the performance reports you have created, provide the information you need to monitor. Careful and consistent monitoring allows you to quickly make adjustments when it is required and to appropriately recognize and thank your employees.

Documenting Results

The following screen displays a set of individual and team performance metrics. These results may be posted daily and weekly. This provides timely opportunities for monitoring performance, coaching, and giving praise and recognition.

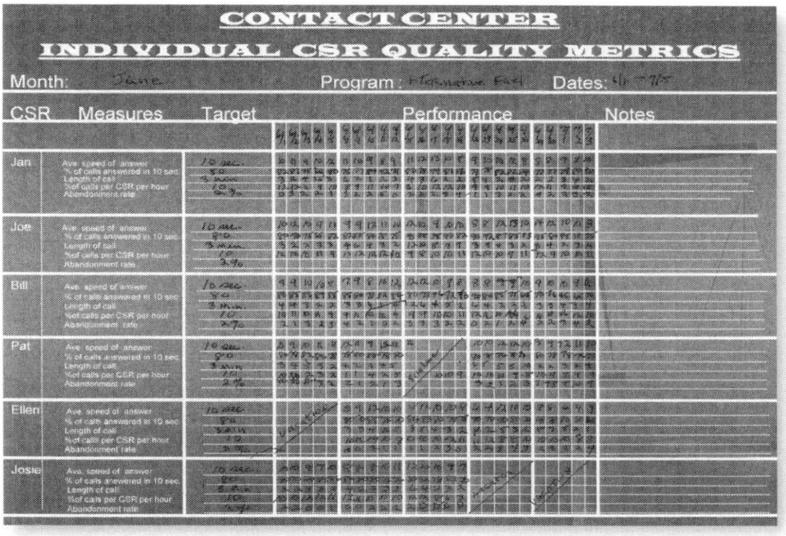

FIGURE 1: Individual Performance

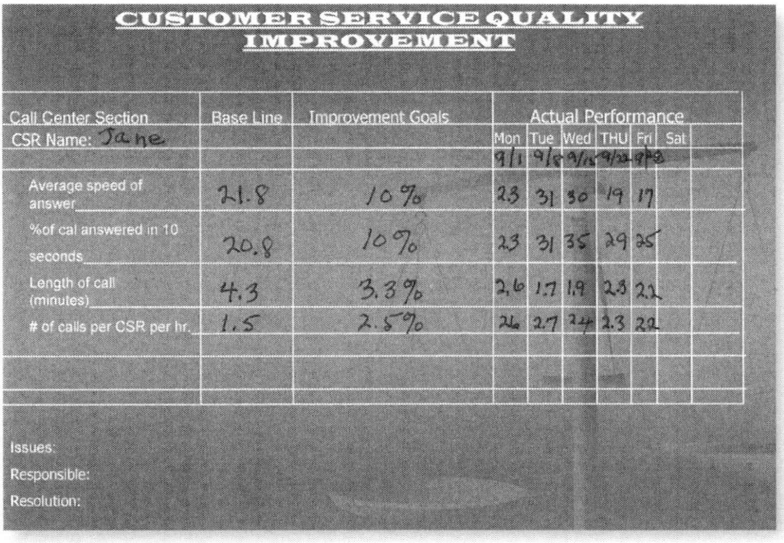

FIGURE 2: Team Performance

The same information that gets used to set goals also gets recalled and used in building an action plan, and then used again in creating feedback loops. It's a one input, multiple use formula of high performance information management. The following is an example of a progress update monitoring screen.

Progress Update Monitoring

Below is an example of how ManagePro summarizes all the progress notes into a concise display for feedback and performance review sessions.

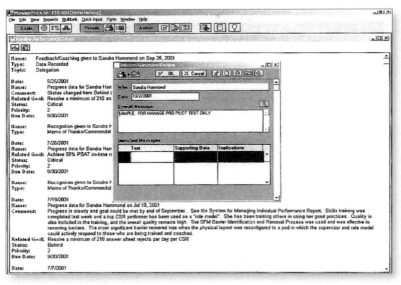

FIGURE 3: ManagePro screen

Periodic Reviews

Periodic and annual reviews are much easier to prepare and are more accurate using ManagePro. Not only does the tool provide a schedule for people managing events, individual goal setting, progress checking, feedback sessions, review sessions, expectation exchanges and commitments, and recognition events, but it also summarizes the progress notes into a concise history for use in reviews. This ensures that the quality of the review goes beyond the last two or three weeks

OPERATIONAL**EXCELLENCE**

and provides details on performance over the entire review period. Following is a view of the "People Status Board," which provides access to the people managing events.

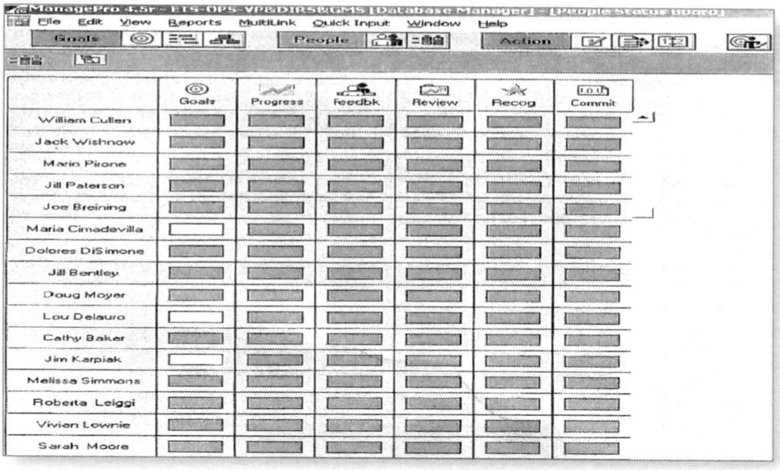

FIGURE 4: Periodic Review

Giving Feedback

You must have accurate information that pertains to the work to be done in order to give meaningful and helpful feedback. Since you will have a metrics system in place to track progress against goals that you and your employees have agreed upon, you will have the relevant information needed for successful feedback.

You will give positive feedback that describes what is on track and why it is on track, and then thank the employee for the good performance. Corrective feedback, which many refer to as negative feedback, can and must be given without being negative. This is a conversation about what is not on track with respect to goal achievement, what the barriers or problems seem to be, and what can be done to get back on track. It is possible that barriers need to be more clearly identified and removed.

You must strive to give feedback often and keep the conversation positive. This is not a time to blame or find fault. It is a time to give feedback, coach and help develop the performance of your employees toward excellence. If you have not been trained in giving feedback, you may want to take a course to develop these valuable skills.

ManagePro provides a context-sensitive "online advisor" to coach a manager with just the right information at just the right time. Following is an example of what the advisor can provide for preparing a feedback session. It is only one click away from the session planner.

Performance Appraisal and Job Description Linkage

Many are confused about the relationships among goals, job descriptions and performance appraisals. Here is some clarification:

Goals are the *what* statements to be accomplished in a specified period of time.

Job descriptions typically are general statements that describe the purpose and parameters of a given job. Rarely are job descriptions specific enough to take the place of goals. Often, job descriptions will describe authority, general responsibilities, spending approval levels and organizational relationships.

Performance appraisals are written once or twice a year for all employees. Research on the success of performance appraisals reveals widespread dissatisfaction on the part of most employees. They believe appraisals do not accurately reflect the work accomplished, do not contain comprehensive measures of performance, and are often written by someone who did not observe the work being accomplished. Business and industry continually strive to develop a performance appraisal system that will be satisfactory.

We believe that performance appraisals are more successful when they are a vital part of a performance management system. To review, a performance management system includes the following:

1. Goal setting, cascading, translating

2. Performance metrics

3. Operating reports

4. Goal and performance documenting

5. Feedback and coaching practices

6. Barrier identification and removal system

7. Reward and recognition program.

When performance appraisals are due, the information required is readily available and comprehensive. The appraisal can then include goal achievement and any other information, such as descriptions of how the work was accomplished. Performance appraisals will take on a new vitality when they are made part of a total performance management system and the human effort is aligned.

1. Reread this chapter with your direct reports' goals in front of you.

2. Review them for content discussed and when your last update was.

3. Gather your direct reports together and summarize this chapter.

4. Review your findings with them and make appropriate changes.

5. Cascade this down to their direct reports and begin to plan for how you will use the information next year.

6. Check the internet for "Management Reporting Systems" to see if you can find a system that will work for you.

7. Review the ManagePro samples included in this chapter with your IT people and inquire about creating your system in-house.

8. Look at ManagePro's website to get far more details about the system than we have given you here.

9. Make a decision about the management information system you will use and get started with it. This is central for operational excellence.

●●● > COMMITMENT CHECK 9

❶ Ask yourself how important the goals are that you have set with people.

❷ Remember your past experiences that may not have helped you improve.

❸ Commit fully to choosing and getting started with a management information system.

❹ Be diligent on measuring performance.

❺ Set your mind to really being diligent on checking progress and giving proper feedback.

The Barrier
Removal Process

10

An integral part of attaining goals is the removal of problems and barriers that are preventing individuals or teams from achieving their goals. It is the responsibility of all employees to identify, document and resolve problems that are preventing them from meeting their goals, and to notify other departments of problems they have identified.

When the problem cannot be resolved at the local level, it is the responsibility of the manager to complete a "barrier removal request" and forward it to the barrier removal coordinator. The coordinator will log the report in a barrier removal log for review in the next management team meeting.

How It Works

Each day, we face problems or barriers that cause our customers to receive less than satisfactory service and us to achieve less than we had planned to achieve. If the problem that we are facing cannot be resolved or eliminated by the local manager, a barrier removal process is needed to resolve the problem and eliminate the barrier. If the local manager cannot remove the barrier, a barrier removal request form will be completed and forwarded to the barrier removal coordinator. The barrier removal coordinator will review the request with the management team and then assign the request for resolution.

How the Barrier Removal Process Works

Identity Barrier	Remove if possible	If not, Record & Submit	Coordinator assigns	Team Removes Barrier	Employee Notified

     The originator of the barrier removal request form will be notified when the barrier removal coordinator assigns a barrier removal team or person to study and remove the barrier. The originator will be notified when the barrier removal coordinator assigns a barrier removal team or person to study and remove the barrier. Also, when the barrier is eliminated the originator will be notified.

The process requires two forms:

1. Barrier removal request form

2. Barrier removal request log.

Samples of both forms are provided on the following two pages.

Barrier Removal Request Form

Originator: _____ Date: _____

Department/Location: _____

Work location phone number: _____

Description of barrier to be removed: _____

_____

_____

_____

_____

Supervisor: _____

Notes: _____

_____

_____

_____

_____

_____

Barrier Removal Request Log

Assigned request number: _____ Date received: _____

Originator: _____ Phone number: _____

Location of barrier: _____

Assigned to: _____ Date assigned: _____

Responsible person's phone number: _____

Date originator and supervisor notified of assignment: _____

Date barrier removed: _____

Date originator and supervisor notified of removal: _____

Notes: _____

_____

_____

_____

_____

_____

WHAT TO DO NOW

1. Set a meeting with your executives and managers to review the barrier removal process and get their commitment to install it.

2. Assign a "champion" to make it happen.

3. Ask the champion to refer to the two sample forms in this chapter and adapt them to your needs.

4. Hold meetings of all employees to announce and "kick off" the process.

COMMITMENT CHECK 10

❶ Are you fully committed to this barrier removal process?

❷ Do you see the value of quickly removing barriers at the location of the barriers?

❸ Adoption of this process will prevent barriers from lingering and interfering with daily work. Do you see the value?

Motivating
Your Employees

11

Important Stuff

Of all the challenges for managers, giving feedback to employees, especially if it is critical, is often difficult. Many managers dread it. We just don't like giving bad news. Consequently, some employees do not get information about behaviors they probably could change until it's too late, and they lose their jobs. Obviously, this is not fair and not appropriate managerial behavior. Managers must step up to the plate and continually give both good news, which we refer to as recognition, and not so good news, which demands improvement. It has been said that so called constructive criticism "scrapes on the way in." However, the long-term consequences are generally positive. All executives, managers and supervisors must develop the skill of giving feedback. With the information available from the reports you have learned about in this handbook and the information you will review in this chapter, even you can do this task well and without dread.

This is one of the most important chapters in the handbook. Please study it carefully and apply the principles right away.

Giving Performance Feedback and Recognition

"The lesson that American Management steadfastly refuses to learn is that managing by emotions, perceptions, or common sense is not really managing at all. Leaders also refuse to accept the fact that people, the very engine of the business machine, cannot be ignored or treated as expendable parts. Human performance is more than a factor in the complicated equation for business success; it is the answer to the equation."

— AUBREY DANIELS

Much has been written about giving recognition and praise. Psychologists call it positive reinforcement. Books abound, some good, some not so good, on the subject of "human motivation." Those of us in management positions are constantly trying to motivate others. *The fact is nobody can motivate anybody to do anything.* However, we can create conditions that invite people to be self-motivated. Motivation can only come from within.

A basic principle is this: "People do what they do, largely because of the consequences." When there is praise or a reward, the behavior probably will be repeated. If punishment or unpleasantness results from the behavior, most people probably will not repeat the behavior. Suppose there is no consequence. When there is superior performance by an employee and no one notices, many will think or say, "What's the use? Nobody cares anyway." We must learn to use the simple tools available to us to invite our employees to be motivated. *Recognition and praise are two of the most basic tools available to us.* Dogs, horses, dolphins, killer whales, and even people can be trained by giving and/or withholding praise and rewards.

As managers and leaders, we must develop a basic understanding of human motivation. The basic techniques of reinforcement and operant conditioning or behavior modification are largely credited to the late Harvard Psychologist B.F. Skinner. In Skinner's experiments, a reinforcement was anything occurring in conjunction with an act that tended to increase the probability the act would happen again, but it was not reward or punishment. It usually comes after an act is completed. Reinforcement occurs during or immediately upon conclusion of the behavior the manager wants to affect. Correctly timed, it changes current behavior and influences future behavior.

There are two categories of reinforcement: positive and negative. A positive reinforcement is something the person wants, such as praise, a heartfelt "thank you," or a pat on the back. A negative reinforcement is something the person wants to avoid, such as a frown, unpleasant comment, or criticism. The effects of negative reinforcement, on the other hand, are not so predictable. Think about the last time you received negative feedback. Did you immediately stop the unacceptable behavior, or did you dig in your heels and stubbornly refuse to change? Did you actually increase the undesired behavior with caution?

Behavior can almost always be intensified with positive reinforcement provided that it is already occurring. You must find a way to get the desired behavior first, usually through training and coaching, and then, reinforce it. Reinforcements are relative, not absolute. A reinforcement must be something the person wants. A reinforcement is information. It communicates. It tells the person exactly what it is you like. In coaching athletes, the coach calls out "Yes!" or "Good!" to mark a move as it occurs. That truly gives the needed information, not the debriefing later in the dressing room. Watching football or other sports, one can see the beautifully timed reinforcements players receive. Reinforcement that arrives too late can be a real problem. The person may not remember the precise behavior being reinforced, so there ends up being little, if any, effect.

The following is an example of reinforcement that can be used in any work center. After improvement goals are set, large team performance charts are created and posted in a prominent place. Performance is posted weekly against current improvement goals. This provides a form of immediate feedback that most employees will anxiously await. Through this simple process, employees can continuously target their efforts toward those areas that need improvement and overall performance will improve. It is critical that supervisors and managers comment upon and thank those who made the increased productivity happen.

This earned recognition will be well received by the employees. After six to eight weeks, the charts should be reconstructed, listing each employee individually. From then on, show weekly performance for each employee. Now the recognition can be more specific and more meaningful. Also under-performing employees can be coached for improvement.

Constant positive reinforcement is only needed in the learning stages. To maintain an already learned behavior, use reinforcement only occasionally. This is what psychologists call a variable schedule. Random, unpredictable reinforcement is far more effective than a constant predictable schedule. This means that you do not have to recognize every employee every day. It is important that the recognition be earned and not a mechanical effort. Let's look at the key points from this brief overview of reinforcement of behavior.

1. Nobody can motivate anybody to do anything. Motivation comes from within and cannot be imposed.

2. We can create conditions that invite people to be self-motivated.

3. People do what they do largely because of the consequences.

4. Recognition, praise and reward are basic tools.

5. Reinforcement is anything occurring in conjunction with an act that tends to increase the probability of the act happening again.

6. Positive reinforcement is something a person wants.

7. Negative reinforcement is something a person wants to avoid.

8. Reinforcement communicates desired behavior.

9. Reinforcement must be timely.

10. Random reinforcement is more effective.

Now let's apply these ten points to the job of managing:

1. **Nobody can motivate anyone to do anything.**
   The motivation switch is on the inside of each of us and only we have access to it. People do what they do for their own reasons, not ours. By the way, at the time we do what we do, it makes sense to us. Later on, in retrospect, some past actions may seem unwise or even stupid. However at the time, the idea seemed pretty good, and

it made sense. The key point is that each of us is in charge of what we do and why we do it. Only I can motivate me, and only you can motivate you. Of course, your employees motivate themselves, and what they do makes perfectly good sense to them.

2. **We can create conditions that invite people to be self-motivated.** What this point says is that we can influence others' actions and invite them to do the things we want. That's what reinforcement, praise and reward is all about. "How can we do this?" you might ask. *The first step is to set clear expectations with each of your employees.* Research shows that the clarity of the job tasks is one of the most important factors in human performance. *Having clear, measurable, challenging goals with due dates is the second most important ingredient in human motivation.* Next come all the important *factors that surround the job.* We must provide good pay and benefits, a safe and pleasant place to work, tools for the job, and excellent training, to name a few. With these conditions in place, we are ready to "catch them doing it right," so we can reinforce the desired behavior. Of course, if these basics are not in place, there is no foundation for reinforcement to work. We must make it inviting for others to do what we want them to do.

3. **People do what they do largely because of the consequences.** An employee just handled a very difficult call from a customer. You listened in on the call. You looked over at her and immediately smiled and gave a "thumbs up" sign. Your employee felt great! She was very glad you were there to hear her do her stuff. That's positive reinforcement. Every time the employee handles a difficult call, that good feeling will come back. Of course, you won't constantly be with her, so you will do the second best thing. You will praise her after her improved performance for the week is posted on the goal and performance charts. If you really want to apply the principles of human motivation, you will praise good performers in front of peers at an appropriate time, such as a meeting. Your recognized and thanked employees will repeat that behavior as often as they can for a lot of reasons, but at the top of the list will be recognition and praise.

As managers, we must take advantage of every opportunity to "catch them doing it right" and to reinforce that behavior. There is no managerial task we have that is more important.

> "*I don't care how great, how famous or successful a man or woman may be, each hungers for APPLAUSE.*"
> — GEORGE M. ADAMS[1]

4. Recognition and praise are basic tools.

A classic book by Bob Nelson, *1001 Ways To Reward Employees*[1], has opened our eyes wide to this subject. When you read the book, which is highly recommended, you will come away with dozens of ideas that are immediately useful. Among the most powerful and most basic are a look in the eye, a squeeze of the hand and a hearty "good job, thank you." How can things so simple be so powerful? It is largely because of our human nature of wanting to be appreciated. *The need to be appreciated is the number one need of most people.* So when you give me a sincere "thank you," you are responding to the foundations of my psyche! *Praise me in front of others and the effect is even more powerful.* We all want to feel good about ourselves. Earned recognition and praise go to the core of the issue. Read Bob Nelson's book for other ideas but put this one into practice now. *By the way, when employees leave a company and they are asked "why" in an exit interview, one of the most frequent answers given is, "I worked my butt off and was not appreciated."* Managers must take advantage of these basic, powerful tools every day at work and at home.

5. A reinforcement is anything occurring in conjunction with an act that tends to increase the probability that the act will happen again.

One thing you can count on: whatever gets rewarded will get done.

In point three above, we gave the example of a manager observing a successful employee call with a difficult customer and immediately giving a "thumbs up." A smile, any encouraging words, a pat on the back, or any idea you can get from Bob Nelson's book will work here. The key point is that this reinforcement has its power because it is given as *the act is occurring*. Dr. Skinner has taught us that this reinforcement is where we really get the payoff. Of course, a basic requirement is that you, as a manager, must allocate your time so you can observe first-hand the performance of your people. You can praise and thank them after the fact, but you can only reinforce while the action is taking place. Office-bound, desk-bound, or computer-bound managers totally miss this important tool. Plan your time to be with your people, observe often and reinforce whenever you can.

6. **Positive reinforcement is something a person wants.**
   You must get to know each one of the people that you manage. You will quickly learn what is important to them. Each person has different needs and wants. They have hobbies, sporting interests, community involvement, family ties, and so on that will tell you what you can do to provide tokens of recognition that fit each person. *Of course, when it comes to praise, one size fits all.* Spend some time finding out just what is wanted and respond with vigor. James Autry, author of *Love and Profit* and former president of *Setter Homes and Garden* magazine, tells about his practice of sending employees congratulation notes on everything from a birthday to a child's graduation to winning a bowling tournament. While it took time and effort for him to discover these events in his employees' lives, the positive impact on morale, performance and retention was tremendous — simple acts with big payoff!

7. **Negative reinforcement is what a person wants to avoid.**
   Negative reinforcement, like criticism, is not very powerful in the behavior change process. However, sometimes we are tempted to provide it. People want to avoid embarrassment at all costs. They also dislike disapproval from significant others like their manager. The safest practice is simply to stay away from negative reinforcement. *It can ruin relationships and trust and it has little power to change behavior.* What more argument do you need to avoid giving negative reinforcement?

8. **Reinforcement communicates the desired behavior.**
   The behavior you desire in your people is learned many ways. You provide formal training, on-the-job training, job descriptions, company and product brochures, procedures manuals, time to observe others who perform similar tasks, and the like. *The most power-*

ful tool in your toolbox, however, is direct observation of the person performing the tasks and giving positive reinforcement for the desired behavior. Often seen as coaching or mentoring, this is an opportunity for the most powerful and precise communication you can possibly give about the behavior you want. This is another strong reason for you to schedule your time carefully and allocate adequate time for this important task.

9. **Reinforcement must be timely.**

As you read earlier, reinforcement must be given as the desired behavior is occurring for it to be effective. After the fact, you can give reward, recognition and/or praise. However, reinforcement changes behavior because it is given during the correct performance of a task. Remember, people do what they do because of what happens to them as they do it. Timely reinforcement is not before or after the performance. It happens during the performance. Make time, observe performance and reinforce the desired performance. That is the formula.

10. **Random reinforcement is more effective.**

If you get in the routine of thanking employees every time you see them, they quickly find out this is just a routine and it has no power. In fact, it can do damage to your credibility. Reinforcement, recognition and praise are more powerful when you are credible, and when they are spontaneous and random. People do not need constant reinforcement to continue excellent performance. Frequency varies with employees' preferences and with managers' preferences. However, excess reinforcement is rarely a problem. The reverse is typically the challenge. All effective managers must become expert at observing behavior and giving random reinforcement. That is how excellence is developed and sustained.

> *"I can live for two months on one good compliment."*
> — MARK TWAIN

These are the principles and some ideas for applying positive reinforcement practices. Make these practices a way of life and you, and those you manage, will experience very positive results.

Step-By-Step Guide for Creating a Recognition Program

1. Implement goal setting, cascading and translation at all levels of the enterprise.

2. Develop and implement metrics so goal attainment can be measured.

3. Measure goal attainment daily, weekly and monthly.

4. Whenever possible, find ways to make goal attainment visible (performance charts).

5. Develop and implement a system for documenting, following up and reviewing goal attainment.

6. Develop and implement a barrier identification and removal system.

7. Conduct training using this chapter as the subject matter. You must be sure all managers understand the role of recognition and are willing to practice what they have read. Agree on the practice you will implement.

8. Have all managers read the book by Bob Nelson, *1001 Ways to Reward Employees*.

9. Appoint a manager of employee recognition (if the size of the enterprise warrants), or assign the responsibility to a human relations specialist to monitor the practice throughout the enterprise and offer counsel, training and other appropriate support.

10. Set a goal for all executives and managers to implement an employee recognition program and make it part of their performance appraisal and bonus program. *Top executives must model the correct practice of employee recognition.*

Productivity and the Self-Fulfilling Prophecy

Years of research and study into these phenomena have produced some startling results. *The expectations that managers have of their employees can and does affect their performance.* When an employee or individual is expected to achieve, it happens. When people are labeled under-achievers, their performance so diminishes. All of us subconsciously communicate our beliefs and expectations to become self-fulfilling prophecies. There are specific behaviors that managers can learn that transmit expectations to instill feelings of value and confidence in all employees.

The managing process presented in this handbook is consistent with the findings of the self-fulfilling prophecy research. The setting of goals at all levels of the organization is the prime example, the goals are SMART, which means change and improvement are built in. The involvement of all employees communicates the expectation that these goals can be achieved. Deadlines are established, metrics are established, and recognition is given for achievement. *Growth and continuous improvement will happen.*

Earl Nightingale, in his presentation "The Strangest Secret," arrives at a similar conclusion. According to Nightingale, *"people become what they think about."* If they think success, they become successful. If they think failure, they fail. People become what they think about all day long. It is the job of managers to implant the ideas and the practices that lead to success in the minds of all employees in order to achieve operational excellence. This is a form of alignment that you read about earlier. The following three pages contain the conclusions of the self-fulfilling prophecy research in headline form. For more information, locate the DVD entitled "Productivity and the Self-Fulfilling Prophecy: The Pygmalion Effect," available from CRM films. The Earl Nightingale DVD is available from Nightingale Conant Company in Chicago. The combination of these two resources will form a powerful foundation for a short course for all managers and supervisors.

Pygmalion in Management
Power of Expectations

- A manager's expectations and treatment of employees largely determine employee performance and career progress.

- A unique characteristic of superior managers is the ability to create high performance expectations that employees fulfill.

- Less effective managers fail to develop similar expectations, and as a consequence, the productivity of their employees suffers.

- Employees, more often than not, appear to do what they believe they are expected to do.

Managers who have been led to expect good results from their employees and others appear to provide the following:

1. **Climate:** The manager sets an accepting, encouraging, social-emotional mood or climate for employees with more potential. This includes warmth, attention, smiling, nodding the head appreciatively — all the positive, nonverbal kinds of communication.

2. **Feedback:** The manager gives these employees more verbal clues about their performance, more reactions, more praise and sometimes even more criticism, all of which help to teach the employee what is needed for improvement.

3. **Input:** The manager will literally teach more material and more difficult material to employees who supposedly have more potential.

4. **Output:** The manager encourages the chosen employees to ask more questions, urges them to respond to the manager's instructions, allows them more time to do a job correctly and gives them the benefit of the doubt.

5

MOTIVATION

People do things for their reasons, not ours…

… and everybody's choices make sense to them at the time.

LAW OF EFFECT

6

(a summary)
E.L.Thorndike, refined by B.F. Skinner

"People's behavior is governed by its consequences."

1. **Positive reinforcement is better than negative.**
2. **Standards or expectations of performance must be clearly defined.**
3. **The leader should reinforce any progress (improvement).**
4. **Stop rewarding undesired behavior either directly or indirectly.**

7

HOW TO GET PEOPLE ACTIVELY INVOLVED

1. Identify specific areas for improvement.
2. Measure daily/weekly performance and post data where everyone can see.
3. Ask people for their ideas for improvement.
4. Recognize individuals and teams for making progress and meeting specific goals.
5. Make everyone feel that they are part of the team.
6. Demonstrate through action that you care about your progress.
7. Make everything you do consistent with your improvement process, each and every day.

A motto: "In partnership with our customers and employees, we will continually investigate and define requirements to assure our products and services always provide total customer satisfaction."

8

The most fundamental need of human beings is to be recognized for their achievements.

WHAT TO DO NOW

1. To the CEO: You need to take the lead on this subject. It is important that all employees at all levels know where you stand on these ideas. We recommend that you make sure you fully understand this chapter. Then write a letter to all employees showing your understanding, your support and your call for this to be a way of life in your organization. Make sure all employees get a copy of your letter. It might be a good idea to send the letter to employees' home addresses so families can be part of this important decision you have made.
2. Ask your director of training or the head of human resources to hold one hour meetings with all executives, managers and supervisors to review this information and reinforce that this will be a way of life at your organization. Exceptions will not be allowed. This could be the start of a cultural change.
3. Request that a recognition program be established and implemented. A task force could accomplish this. Choose a leader and set a due date.

COMMITMENT CHECK **11**

1. I understand the principles learned/reviewed in this chapter and agree to make sure all executives, managers and supervisors do also.
2. I will model these behaviors to the best of my ability and give feedback and/or recognition to others as I observe their behavior. Negative behavior will not be tolerated and will be promptly corrected.
3. You will demonstrate your commitment to accomplishing the three points above in "WHAT TO DO NOW".
4. However, your most powerful commitment will be demonstrated as you "walk the talk."

REFERENCES

[1] Nelson, Bob, "1001 Ways to Reward Employees", Workman Publishing ©1994.
[2] Adams, George M., American Author 1878-1962, Cybernation.com, Quote Center.

A Very Small Textbook for Managing People

12

Over the years, my colleagues and I have conducted dozens of seminars, workshops and training sessions on most of the subjects that relate to managing people. One of the simple exercises we do involves asking our participants to brainstorm and complete two sentences. Below are the results. It is a composite list of the comments most often made.

I've done my *best* work for bosses who…	I've done my *worst* work for bosses who…
Commit	Are closed minded
Respect me	Don't communicate
Communicate with me	Are selfish
Appreciate me	Are disrespectful
Involve themselves	Threaten and intimidate
Care about what they do	Blame others
Support me	Are self-centered
Are willing to listen	Are dictatorial
Are consistent	Have their own agendas
Understand me	Criticize behind your back
Are honest	Second guess you
Lead by example	Won't commit
Are open-minded	Ignore me
Set clear goals	Are indecisive
Set expectations	Are ill-tempered
continued…	*continued…*

I've done my *best* work for bosses who…	I've done my *worst* work for bosses who…
Give recognition	Are dishonest
Teach us what we need	Are egotistical
Trust us	Are hard-liners
Give rewards	Don't appreciate workers
Encourage me	Are overly demanding
Are professional	Steal credit
Are approachable and open	Lie
Act humanely	Won't take responsibility
Have a good temperament	Provide little direction
Maintain composure	Are unseen
	Do not think "safety first"

Please read these lists carefully and thoughtfully. What would you have added if you were in one of these sessions? Which column most describes you? If you are not sure, ask a trusted colleague or two to review the list and put a checkmark by the items that describe you. Then, thoughtfully review that feedback and decide if there are any changes you need to make. Then, find a way to get the training, education and coaching you might need. You can find dozens of opportunities on the internet. Just search for "management training." You will find seminars, books, short courses, DVDs, videotapes, college and university online courses, and lots of other stuff you may not have thought about.

Unfortunately, these subjects are outside the goals of this handbook but are so necessary that we wanted to bring them to your attention and give a little advice.

LEADERSHIP

Definition: The skill of influencing people to enthusiastically work toward goals identified as being for the common good.

Leadership is *not* management.

Management is made up of the things we do: plan, organize, staff, delegate, follow-up, report.

Leadership is *who we are.*

Leaders are effective communicators.

An effective leader will exhibit these characteristics:

- Moral authority
- The ability to tell and show
- Patience
- Kindness
- Humility
- Respect for others

- Selflessness
- Forgiveness
- Honesty
- Trust
- Accountability

Where do you stand in these areas?

WHAT TO DO NOW

1. Plan to combine this short chapter with the session we recommend for Chapter 11.

2. During the session, the classroom leader may ask the attendees to review the two lists and put a checkmark beside the entries that are relevant for them. Also, ask them to add any items they care to.

3. A lively classroom discussion will typically follow these two assignments.

4. Conclude the discussion by re-emphasizing the relevance and seriousness of the small piece of information.

5. Hold a discussion on Power Punch #9, "Leadership," and again emphasize the relevance.

●●❯ COMMITMENT CHECK 12

❶ Chapter 11 and Chapter 12 are critically important. What these chapters teach is mandatory for a positive implementation of operational excellence. Also, these behaviors should become a way of life for all executives, managers and associates of your enterprise.

❷ Do you believe this?

❸ Are you committed to make this happen?

Training for Excellence 13

How Adults Learn

Introduction

To prepare you for the training program's planning, purchasing and/or designing process, we want to review the principles of how adults learn. These principles form the foundation for any program you may consider as you undertake operational excellence.

There is an old saying that "if somebody needs to learn to tell time, they don't need to learn how to build a clock." We often err on the side of teaching too much or the wrong information. Adults want to learn only what they need *now* and not something else. This chapter will teach you how to do just that.

The relationship between learning theory and the practical aspects of training is often a matter of debate. Some people insist that good training depends on a thorough knowledge of learning theory and principles. Others believe that theory is not very helpful in any business situation, including training. Both positions have some validity.

Learning theory rarely provides direct answers to training program designers', instructors', managers' and/or program participants' questions. Yet, any serious consideration of training techniques must begin with a common understanding of learning principles.

This brief presentation is based on a conviction that learning and training depend on each other. We define training as a set of procedures that are meant to cause learning. Anyone who successfully offers training programs must know and respond to these procedures.

The presentation is organized around four major topics:

1. Basic principles of learning

2. Conditions that make learning easier

3. Characteristics of adult learning

4. Fundamental training processes.

1. Principles of Learning

In many ways, training can be compared with the art of fishing. The lure and other paraphernalia are designed to catch the eye of the fisherman, but not necessarily the fish! Likewise, many so called training programs are designed to the style of the instructor. They "cover information," "tell how," or "show how." It is sometimes difficult to tell whether there is any real relationship between the teaching techniques and the learning taking place. Often the learner can describe the instructor's style, humor, or presentation skills, but cannot remember or use the presented information.

At times, the teaching appears to succeed. However, experience tells us that in many cases, teaching is probably unimportant. *Learning can and does happen without it.* As you study the information that follows, you will see that the role of the instructor has shifted from being subject matter-oriented to being *learner-, problem-, and process-oriented.*

1. Learning is an experience that happens within the learner. The learner is in charge.

2. Meaningful learning is more permanent and transferable than learning that consists of memorized facts.

3. Adult learners learn what they do.

4. Learning is a cooperative process between the instructor and the adult learner.

5. Among the richest resources for learning are the adult learners themselves.

6. Learning requires change, and change is sometimes resisted.

7. Adults prefer to take short, focused courses for immediate application.

8. Learning takes time. It takes place gradually.

9. Learning proceeds most effectively when the adult learner receives immediate feedback on responses.

10. There are different kinds of learning and they require different training processes.

2. Conditions That Make Learning Easier

In addition to the fundamental principles that govern learning, instructors need to recognize the impact of *surrounding conditions*. Basically, we need to address the influence of atmosphere and attitudes that aid in achieving the training objectives.

"Conditions that make learning easier" can be organized into two categories: conditions that relate to a "sense of *acceptance*," and conditions that relate to a "sense of freedom" within the learning situation. The following conditions that make learning easier can be grouped under these two categories:

a. Sense of acceptance

- ► Learning is made easier in an atmosphere where people feel accepted.

- ► Learning is made easier in an atmosphere that honors and shares the learner's, as well as the instructor's, background, experience and perspective.

- ► Learning is made easier in an atmosphere in which difference of opinion is considered good and desirable.

- ► Learning is made easier in an atmosphere that consistently recognizes people's rights to make mistakes and not be criticized.

- ► Learning is made easier when learners are not embarrassed by their individual performance.

b. Sense of freedom

- ► Learning is made easier in an atmosphere that encourages people to be active.

- Learning is made easier in an atmosphere where the evaluation emphasis is on self-evaluation.
- Learning is made easier when learners are free to question other class members and the instructor, as well as be questioned by other class members and the instructor.
- Learning is made easier when the learning objectives are clear and the instructor's methods encourage active learning through practice.
- Learning is made easier when learners have fun and enjoy the learning process.

3. Characteristics of Adult Learning

Given the principles of learning and the supporting conditions we have presented, it is clear that the teaching process is important to the learning process. The definition of "teaching" adults, however, needs to be examined. Traditional approaches to adult training were based on assumptions derived from outdated principles of youth education. Adult learners have at least four characteristics that differ from these outdated ideas. An awareness of the expectations of adult learners will add another important dimension to your understanding. What are these expectations? What are the implications for helping adults to learn?

- Adults have a need to be treated with respect and not be embarrassed.
- Adults have accumulated experiences and need to share them.
- Adults are not always ready to learn. They must see a need.
- Time perspective is shorter for adults. They want information they can use now.

4. The Fundamental Process of Training

The following four fundamental training processes are derived from the principles, conditions and characteristics of adult learning. These principles, conditions and characteristics describe the learning environment and provide critical inputs for training decisions. Acknowledging the principles, conditions and characteristics helps the training program designer and the instructor commit to using the appropriate processes.

The four processes are:

1. Guidance and reinforcement: Lead adult learners through carefully prepared course materials containing clear objectives, and give ongoing positive reinforcement.

2. Association: Be sure to relate new ideas to information already known. Also, relate to the need for what is being learned.

3. Active participation: Learners should be actively engaged in all learning activities.

4. Provide opportunities: Give learners the chance to practice and apply newly acquired knowledge.

An Important Summary About How Adults Learn

Learning will happen with or without teaching! Good teaching, however, gives you an opportunity to teach the right stuff. When employees learn on their own, they pick up both good and bad techniques and information. Good training is critical for operational excellence to happen.

Remember that adults typically want to learn what they need now. Additional stuff will be promptly dismissed or forgotten. This means you must do a careful analysis of needs before you decide what the training program will contain. Please use the guide we have provided.

Adults learn what they do. So here is what you must do:

1. Tell them.

2. Tell them what you told them.

3. Show them.

4. Let them practice until they get it or, in the case of a skill, they can do it.

5. Note this: If they can do it in the classroom, they probably can do it on the job. If they have no opportunity to practice in the classroom, don't expect correct on-the-job performance. This is especially true for skill building.

6. Adults are not always ready to learn. They must see a need. Make this part of your learning design.

7. As you will see in "The Curve of Forgetting" that follows, most adults have a short memory span. So train just before the employees need the new information or skill, or they might forget what they learned.

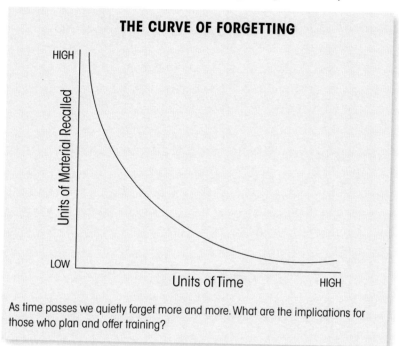

THE CURVE OF FORGETTING

HIGH

Units of Material Recalled

LOW

Units of Time   HIGH

As time passes we quietly forget more and more. What are the implications for those who plan and offer training?

As you design, develop and implement training programs for adults, be certain to follow the guidelines offered here to help assure success.

Types Of Learning

Human behavior can be viewed as consisting of three major aspects: knowledge, skills and attitude. To be effective, training must address all three: what the learner *knows, needs to know, can do, must learn to do* and how the learner *feels.*

Knowledge refers to facts, concepts, principles, rules, or policies that contain information or subject matter that the learner needs to acquire. Some knowledge must be memorized and some can be looked up when required. One must only need to know where and how to locate and use the needed information.

Skills refer to the learner's ability to do things, either with the head (mentally) or with the hands (physically). Skills can be primarily cognitive (solving a problem, applying a principle, making a decision) or manual (assembling, operating a computer, demonstrating a product, repairing something).

Attitude is an individual's positive or negative reaction toward some person, thing, or situation (how they feel).

The Relationship of These Three

Categories of human behavior can be shown as a triangle. Each side is dependent upon the others to be effective. In other words, all three must be present to get the desired result.

Determining Training Needs: A Guide

As you read earlier about how adults learn, adults are not always ready to learn. They must see a need for acquiring the new knowledge and skills. They want information they can use immediately. Training designs that respond to this fact are built upon a foundation of learner needs. Therefore, training program designers require a process for determining training needs. The guide that follows will serve you well.

This "Determining Training Needs" guide is based on the work of Robert F. Mager and Peter Pipe, as described in their book, **Analyzing Performance Problems,**[1] *©1970. The checklist that follows is from that book and used with permission of the publisher.*

Categories of Questions to Answer	Questions to Ask
I. They aren't doing what they should be doing. I think I've got a training problem. 1. What is the performance discrepancy? 2. Is it a skill deficiency?	▸ What is the difference between current results and what you expect? ▸ When did the performance decline? ▸ Could they do it if they really had to? ▸ Could they do it if their lives depended upon it? ▸ Are their present skills adequate for the desired performance?
II. Yes. It is a skill deficiency. They couldn't do it if their lives depended on it. 3. Could they do it in the past? 4. Is the skill used often? 5. Do they have what it takes?	▸ Did they once know how to perform, as you desire? ▸ Have they forgotten how to do what you want them to do? ▸ How often is the skill or performance used? ▸ Do they get regular feedback about how well they perform? ▸ Exactly how do they find out how well they are doing? ▸ Can they learn the job? ▸ Do they have the physical and mental potential to perform as you desire?

III. It is not a skill deficiency. They could do it if they wanted to.

6. Is the desired performance punishing?

7. Is non-performance rewarding?

8. Are there obstacles to performing?

- What is the consequence of performing as desired?
- Is it punishing to perform as expected? (i.e.: additional time, hassle, not income producing)
- What is the result of doing it their way instead of your way?
- What do they get out of present performance (reward)?
- What prevents them from performing?
- Do they know what is expected of them?

IV. What should you do now?

9. What solution is best?

10. Develop a plan with your recommendations and present it to the appropriate leader in the organization.

- Are any possible solutions inappropriate or impossible to implement?
- Are any solutions plainly beyond your resources?
- What would it "cost" for the preferred solution? What would be the added value if you implemented the preferred solution?

Following are some ideas for you to consider as you develop a plan for the person who requested the training program.

1. Be sure you understand the performance discrepancy. For example, the expectation is a monthly average sales volume of $200,00 per salesperson. The actual is $175,000.

2. If the salespeople can meet the performance expectations if their lives depend on it, there is no training needed. However, there may be other needs such as product availability, product quality, salesperson motivation, and the like. You probably cannot impact these variables with training.

3. If the salespeople could meet performance expectations in the past, you may consider refresher training. However, they may also need a job aid — a set of detailed instructions — to be used as a reference. It is easy to forget how to do something you do infrequently.

4. You may have to trade your "trainer" hat for an "organization development" hat. You may have to deal with obstacles to performance that are not directly related to training.

●●●❯ COMMITMENT CHECK **13**

❶ Since adults learn best by "doing" you will always allow discussion and practice in the classroom.

❷ You will provide short training sessions just before the skills and information are required to prevent forgetting.

❸ You will always determine precise needs before offering training.

❹ You will stimulate and allow questions and discussion in all classroom sessions.

❺ You will always invite everyone to participate.

❻ Bring the donuts and coffee.

REFERENCES

[1]Mager, Robert F. and Pipe, Peter, "Analyzing Performance Problems," Fearon Publishers, ©1970, Ref. pages 101-105.

OPERATIONAL**EXCELLENCE**

Conducting
Effective Meetings

14

Anthony Jay, a producer of training films for industry, reported the results of a study with 1,000 executives and managers regarding their experience with meetings. The major findings were these:

- Most believe they spend too much time in meetings.
- They believe that at least one third of their time in meetings is non-productive.
- Many are frustrated, bored and consider the meeting a waste of time.
- Top executives believe that running a meeting is a crucial test of a manager's ability.
- Good meetings are good management. Everyone is sent off with understanding and a sense of purpose. This is when a manager is seen as a leader, skilled at running meetings.
- Bad meetings send attendees off de-motivated, irritated and alienated. People who run bad meetings usually do not improve. Worse than that, they pass on their bad habits to those who attend their bad meetings.

There is hope. Holding meetings is a management skill and can be learned. The information that follows is what good meetings are all about.

1. Plan

2. Inform others

3. Create an orderly agenda and prepare

4. Maintain full control of the discussions

5. Summarize and record

Let's look at the details of each of the five elements:

1. Plan

First, ask why you want to hold this meeting. What outcome do you want? Write an agenda. Do you really need to hold this meeting or can the outcome you want be attained another way? Possibly the telephone, a conference call, e-mail, or even one-to-one communication will get what you need.

Be sure your agenda is intelligent and orderly. Put the important items first. You will allot more time to these. The important topics may also be the most urgent. If not, put the urgent items first and then list other items in the order of importance. Your agenda should not just be a list of topics. You should give a brief explanation of what the problem or opportunity is and the outcome you want to achieve. List an estimated time allocation for each item on the agenda. Then, determine the meeting ending time. Record this information on the agenda.

Then, make sure that the right people are invited to the meeting. These are people with knowledge to contribute and may have a large stake in the outcome. Select someone to record the major points of the meeting and those who will be responsible for action items.

2. Inform Others

Send your meeting invitation and an agenda to each person who should attend. Ask them to come fully prepared to deal with the topics on the agenda.

With these two steps completed, you have set the stage for a successful meeting.

3. Create an Orderly Agenda and Prepare

The agenda is so important that we listed it again. However, the purpose of this step is for you to fully prepare for the meeting. You know the outcomes you want. Make sure you have all the resources you need, both information and people.

4. Maintain Full Control of the Discussions

Control begins by starting on time and ending on time. Be sure everybody stays on the topic being worked. Do not allow side conversations or non-value-added discussion. Do this:

- ► Announce the topic
- ► Discuss the announced topic only
- ► Arrive at a conclusion
- ► Make a decision
- ► Record your decision
- ► Move on to the next topic
- ► Critique your meeting

5. Summarize and Record

You may do this at the conclusion of each topic or at the end of the meeting. Be sure to record all decisions, all actions that must be taken, the names of those responsible for the actions and due dates.

In Conclusion

Now doesn't this make sense? It is an easy-to-understand process that can be learned by most people. To further assist you, we have provided a meeting planning guide and a critique sheet for all attendees to complete at the conclusion of the meeting. Be sure to allow time for this critique. You will be amazed at how soon and how much your meetings will improve.

Meeting Guide
Planning the meeting

1. Determine the purpose of the meeting.

2. Write an agenda.

3. The agenda needs to be in a logical order.

4. Determine who needs to attend.

5. Set an approximate time limit for each item.

6. Determine the overall length of the meeting.

7. Set the date, time and location.

8. Determine who will be the recorder for the meeting.

9. Send invitations that include the purpose of the meeting and an agenda.

Conducting the meeting

1. Start the meeting on time.

2. State what needs to be accomplished.

3. Follow the agenda.

4. Hold appropriate discussions.

5. Reach a conclusion (or determine if additional information is required and set a follow-up meeting).

6. Make necessary decisions and determine action steps.

7. Record who is responsible for each action and the due dates.

8. Critique the meeting.

9. Adjourn on time.

Meeting Critique

The purpose of the critique is improving the quality of your meetings. Please be candid with your evaluation and critique. Most responses will be "yes" or "no." Comments can be valuable to the meeting leader.

_____ 1. I got the agenda ahead of time.

_____ 2. The meeting started on time.

_____ 3. The leader stated what needed to be accomplished.

_____ 4. The leader followed the agenda.

_____ 5. Discussions were kept on the topic.

_____ 6. We appropriately reached a conclusion.

_____ 7. We did not reach a conclusion, but planned next steps.

_____ 8. We decided who is responsible for each action step.

_____ 9. We set due dates for all action items.

_____ 10. We critiqued the meeting.

_____ 11. We adjourned on time.

Comments:

_____

_____

_____

_____

Department Meeting Matrix

You must complete a meeting matrix for your department or section for which you are responsible. A sample matrix is shown on the next three pages. This is a great communications tool. Also, as you begin to practice the lessons learned in this chapter, you may be able to eliminate some of these meetings. If it is a must-have meeting, keep it. If the meeting covers "old stuff," and it is not vital, or you can accomplish this communication another way, cancel it. You will be surprised how much time and effort is spent in meetings when your meeting matrix is completed. This is an excellent way to identify and remove some non-value-added work.

Plant Communications Matrix
Daily/Weekly Meetings

	Mon	Tues	Wed	Thu	Fri
7-8	STOM	STOM	STOM	STOM	STOM
8:30-9:15	MCM	MCM	MCM	MCM	MCM
9-11			RACAPA	Commitment	
1-3			Process sectional meeting		
3-4	STOM	STOM	STOM	STOM	STOM
3-5		Prod. Monthly Meeting			Process Review
11-12	STOM	STOM	STOM	STOM	STOM

Meeting	Schedule	Meeting Agenda	Attendees
STOM	Last hour of every shift	Turn-over of pending jobs and priorities for the next shift	All Shift supervisors, add daytime supervisors if during the day
MCM	Every morning, 8:30-9:15 and telecons every Sat at 10am	Coordination of SMD, plant requirements and Quarry support Review/revision of short-term plans	Logistics Supervisor, Plant Manager, Quarry Manager, Production Manager, Maintenance Manager, QA Manager
RACAPA	Every Wed, 10-12	Root cause analysis and corrective/preventive actions for equipment downtimes	Plant: Maintenance Manager, Production Manager, Production Supt., Prev Maint Supt, Elect Supt, IA Supt. Quarry: Quarry Manager, QCO Supt, Head of C/M
Commitment	Every Thur, 10-12	Prioritization of M2 Notifications, Scheduling of PM's	Plant: Production Mgr, Maint Mgr, Supts. Quarry: Quarry Manager, QCO Supt, Head of C/M Maintenance
CSC	2nd working day after HIP Report is released. HIP Report is usually released by the 4th of the month	Review of OH&S Performance, Incidents, Non-Conformances and Corrective/Preventive Actions	Members of the CSC
MRM	2nd working day after HIP Report is released. HIP Report is usually released by the 4th of the month	Review of Plant KPI's, Projections, Inter-Department Issues	Department Managers, Environment Officer
Project Review	Every 3rd Tues of the month	Review of progress of capex and projects, approval of proposed M1 Projects	Plant Manager, Maintenance Manager, Production Manager, Project Leaders
Support Actions Review	Every 4th Wed of the month	Review of Support Actions and re-prioritization of support actions	Department Managers
Safety Notifications Meeting	Every 2nd Mon of the month	Prioritization of Safety Notifications, Progress Review of Safety Work Orders	OH&S Officer, Engineering Superintendent, Electrical Supt, Safety Inspector, Production Supt, Union Reps
Business Briefings	Every quarter as scheduled by Mancom	Review of company performance, developments and interaction with Mancom	All Plant Employees
IMS Management Rev	Every semester as scheduled by the IMR	Review of IMS (as per Management Review Policy)	All Department Managers, OH&S Rep, Environment Rep, Quality Rep
MRFC	Every quarter as scheduled by the MRFC	MRFC Minutes, OH&S Performance, Environment Performance, SMDP Report	All Department Managers, Environment Officer, OH&S Officer, Quarry Planner plus external members of MRFC
Quality Review	Every quarter as scheduled by QA Manager	SMD-Plant meeting to review customer feedback, quality performance and plan on corrective/preventive actions	Plant Manager, QA Manager, Production Manager, SMD Product Manager
Performance Support Planning Workshop	Every December as scheduled by the Plant Manager	Review of action plans to support next year's budget	Department Managers and selected supts, supervisors and associates
Weekly Process Sectional Meeting	Every Wed, 1-3	Review previous week's plant performance of raw mills, kiln and cement mills and create action plans to improve efficiency if needed	Process Head, Process Engineers

FIGURE 1: This is an example of a plant wide schedule of all planned meetings. It serves as an excellent communications tool.

Plant Maintenance Department Communications Matrix
Daily/Weekly Meetings

Time	Mon	Tues	Wed	Thu	Fri	Sat	Sun
7-8	STOM	STOM	STOM	STOM	STOM		
8-8:30	DPRM	DPRM	DPRM	DPRM	DPRM	DPRM	DPRM
8:30-9:15	MCM	MCM	MCM	MCM	MCM		
9-11			RACAPA	Commitment			
10-11	DMRM	DMRM			DMRM		
10-12			RACAPA	Commitment			
2-3					SPS		
3-4	STOM	STOM	STOM	STOM	STOM		
3-5					Process Review		
7:55-8am, 3:55-4pm, 11:55-12mn	DSTOM	DSTOM	DSTOM	DSTOM	DSTOM	DSTOM	DSTOM
11-12	STOM	STOM	STOM	STOM	STOM		

Meeting	Schedule	Meeting Agenda	Attendees
STOM - Shift Turnover Meeting	Last hour of every shift	Turn-over of pending jobs and priorities for the next shift	All Shift supervisors, add daytime supervisors if during the day
MCM – Manager's Coordination Meeting	Every morning, 8:30-9:15 and telecons every Sat at 10am	Coordination of SMD, plant requirements and Quarry support Review/revision of short-term plans	Logistics Supervisor, Plant Manager, Quarry Manager, Production Manager, Maintenance Manager, QA Manager
RACAPA – Remedial Action, Corrective Action, Preventive Action	Every Wed, 10-12	Root cause analysis and corrective/preventive actions for equipment downtimes	Plant: Maintenance Manager, Production Manager, Production Supt., Prev Maint Supt, Elect Supt, IA Supt. Quarry: Quarry Manager, QCO Supt, Head of C/M
Weekly Commitment Meeting	Every Thur, 10-12	Prioritization of M2 Notifications, Scheduling of PM's	Plant: Production Mgr, Maint Mgr, Supts. Quarry: Quarry Manager, QCO Supt, Head of C/M Maintenance
CSC – Central Safety Committee	2nd working day after HIP Report is released. HIP Report is usually released by the 4th of the month	Review of OH&S Performance, Incidents, Non-Conformances and Corrective/Preventive Actions	Members of the CSC
MRM – Monthly Review Meeting	2nd working day after HIP Report is released. HIP Report is usually released by the 4th of the month	Review of Plant KPI's, Projections, Inter-Department Issues	Department Managers, Environment Officer
Project Review	Every 3rd Tues of the month	Review of progress of capex and projects, approval of proposed M1 Projects	Plant Manager, Maintenance Manager, Production Manager, Project Leaders
Support Actions Review	Every 4th Wed of the month	Review of Support Actions and re-prioritization of support actions	Department Managers
Safety Notifications Meeting	Every 2nd Mon of the month	Prioritization of Safety Notifications, Progress Review of Safety Work Orders	OH&S Officer, Engineering Superintendent, Electrical Supt, Safety Inspector, Production Supt, Union Reps
Business Briefings	Every quarter as scheduled by Mancom	Review of company performance, developments and interaction with Mancom	All Plant Employees
IMS Management Reviews	Every semester as scheduled by the IMR	Review of IMS (as per Management Review Policy)	All Department Managers, OH&S Rep, Environment Rep, Quality Rep
MRFC	Every quarter as scheduled by the MRFC	MRFC Minutes, OH&S Performance, Environment Performance, SMDP Report	All Department Managers, Environment Officer, OH&S Officer, Quarry Planner plus external members of MRFC
Performance Support Planning Workshop	Every December as scheduled by the Plant Manager	Review of action plans to support next year's budget	Department Managers and selected supts, supervisors and associates
Daily Planning & Review Meeting	Daily during 2nd shift, 8-8:30am held in each work center	Review previous day's events, dispatching of work orders and review of daily action logs	Maintenance Supt., Planners and Associates
Daily Maintenance Review Meeting	Daily during 2nd shift, 10-11am held at the 4th flr MPR rm	Review of maintenance action logs, coordination of activities between work centers, prioritization of activities, maintenance cost review, communication of plant mancom decisions and concerns	Maintenance Manager, All Maintenance Supt.
Departmental Shift Turn Over Meeting	Every end of shift for Mechanical, Electrical, Instrumentation and Lubrication	Turn-over of pending jobs and priorities for the next shift per work center	Incoming and Outgoing Shift Associates and Supervisors
SPS Meeting	Every Friday	Review of SPS requirement	Production, MM, Maintenance Supts.

FIGURE 2: This is an example of all planned maintenance meetings. It serves as an excellent planning and communications tool.

Daily/Weekly Meetings

	Mon	Tues	Wed	Thu	Fri
7-8	STOM	STOM	STOM	STOM	STOM
8:30-9:15	MCM	MCM	MCM	MCM	MCM
9-11			RACAPA	Commitment	
3-4	STOM	STOM	STOM	STOM	STOM
3-5					Process Review
11-12	STOM	STOM	STOM	STOM	STOM

Meeting	Schedule	Meeting Agenda	Attendees
STOM	Last hour of every shift	Turn-over of pending jobs and priorities for the next shift	All Shift supervisors, add daytime supervisors if during the day
MCM	Every morning, 8:30-9:15 and telecons every Sat at 10am	Coordination of SMD, plant requirements and Quarry support Review/revision of short-term plans	Logistics Supervisor, Plant Manager, Quarry Manager, Production Manager, Maintenance Manager, QA Manager
RACAPA	Every Wed, 10-12	Root cause analysis and corrective/ preventive actions for equipment downtimes	Plant: Maintenance Manager, Production Manager, Production Supt., Prev Maint Supt, Elect Supt, IA Supt. Quarry: Quarry Manager, QCO Supt, Head of C/M
Commitment	Every Thur, 10-12	Prioritization of M2 Notifications, Scheduling of PM's	Plant: Production Mgr, Maint Mgr, Supts. Quarry: Quarry Manager, QCO Supt, Head of C/M Maintenance
CSC	2nd working day after HIP Report is released. HIP Report is usually released by the 4th of the month	Review of OH&S Performance, Incidents, Non-Conformances and Corrective/Preventive Actions	Members of the CSC
MRM	2nd working day after HIP Report is released. HIP Report is usually released by the 4th of the month	Review of Plant KPI's, Projections, Inter-Department Issues	Department Managers, Environment Officer
Project Review	Every 3rd Tues of the month	Review of progress of capex and projects, approval of proposed M1 Projects	Plant Manager, Maintenance Manager, Production Manager, Project Leaders
Support Actions Review	Every 4th Wed of the month	Review of Support Actions and re-prioritization of support actions	Department Managers
Safety Notifications Meeting	Every 2nd Mon of the month	Prioritization of Safety Notifications, Progress Review of Safety Work Orders	OH&S Officer, Engineering Superintendent, Electrical Supt, Supt., Safety Inspector, Production Supt, Union Reps
Business Briefings	Every quarter as scheduled by Mancom	Review of company performance, developments and interaction with Mancom	All Plant Employees
IMS Management Rev	Every semester as scheduled by the IMR	Review of IMS (as per Management Review Policy)	All Department Managers, OH&S Rep, Environment Rep, Quality Rep
MRFC	Every quarter as scheduled by the MRFC	MRFC Minutes, OH&S Performance, Environment Performance, SMDP Report	All Department Managers, Environment Officer, OH&S Officer, Quarry Planner plus external members of MRFC
Quality Review	Every quarter as scheduled by QA Manager	SMD-Plant meeting to review customer feedback, quality performance and plan on corrective/ preventive actions	Plant Manager, QA Manager, Production Manager, SMD Product Manager
Performance Support Planning Workshop	Every December as scheduled by the Plant Manager	Review of action plans to support next year's budget	Department Managers and selected supts, supervisors and associates

FIGURE 3: This is an example of all planned maintenance meetings. It serves as an excellent planning and communications tool.

To the CEO:

1. Ask several of your executives and managers to read this short instruction on holding effective meetings.

2. Then, ask them to use the meeting critique sheet to evaluate several meetings they will attend. We suggest you get about a dozen critiques.

3. Have a knowledgeable person create a meeting matrix for you.

4. Then, call a meeting of those who critiqued meetings and determine the effectiveness and quality of meetings being conducted in your organization. In this same meeting, show and discuss the meeting matrix and determine if some changes can be made.

5. You will probably find that some level of improvement is in order.

6. If that is so, assign this short reading to all in your organization who conduct meetings.

7. Tell the meeting leaders that this process is being adopted organization-wide, and you expect all meetings to be conducted according to the plan presented in the reading assignment.

8. Follow-up by reading the critiques from your meetings and a selection of other critiques as well.

9. Follow-up with the meeting matrix task and eliminate all the meetings that you can.

●●◉ COMMITMENT CHECK 14

❶ I agree to determine the quality of the meetings held at various levels of the organization.

❷ Then, I will decide if some change is in order.

❸ I will work with the meeting matrix to make necessary refinements.

❹ If change is needed, I will follow the steps given to me above.

Putting It All Together 15

Assessing the Gap

Now that you have developed your vision for the future and set your goals in that direction, you are ready to assess the gap between now and then or the current and future state. This will allow you to clearly define or refine your business plan.

Operational excellence means different things to different organizations. A sales organization looks for best practices for sales. A consulting firm looks at best practices for consulting. For purposes of this book, we will use examples from our fictional company to help set the stage. Does any of this look familiar?

Their maintenance and operations costs are too high, and they are not able to ship all their products on time. If they could increase overall equipment effectiveness (OEE) from 78% to 81%, *this would mean an increase of 12 million dollars and better customer satisfaction.* That doesn't appear to be a large increase, and it may seem easy, but this is more difficult than it sounds.

They have an entrenched culture and an aging workforce. The plant is highly reactive and complicated to run. There have been many additions and upgrades, but no consistency in engineering standards or processes. There are three production lines, but two are quite old. The third one is newer, but it is still thirty years old. The product they make tends to be more of an art then a science. Here are some of their overall performance indicators:

- OEE = 78%
- Production rate = 95%
- Uptime = 88%
- First pass quality= 94%
- Maintenance schedule compliance = 45%
- Emergency work = 35%
- Maintenance costs as a percentage of equipment replacement value = 20.5%
- Average increase of maintenance costs annually over 8 years = 10%
- Stores efficiency = 65%
- Overtime = 25%
- Contractor costs = HIGH
- Capital needed to maintain percentage of EBITDA = HIGH, but not provided

There are many good books on metrics and best practices, such as Terry Wireman's *Developing Performance Indicators for Managing Maintenance*. There are models like the pillars or the arch. The most common one is the pyramid. In all model types, the concept is always the same. You must lay the foundation and build up. We are showing an assessment tool that is shaped like a house. The elements tend to always be similar as well. The place to start is to understand your current practices. Now that we know where we are we can start.

The most common mistake is to overlook the fact that the plant is running and making money. It is just that there is more money to be made. This makes it difficult for companies. They do not have a compelling story of bankruptcy or closure. They must focus on improving the bottom line and staying competitive while continuing to protect the quality of life of the employees.

This means there must be some good things taking place. Employees have a certain amount of pride and ownership. If you completely discount this, you are missing one of your most helpful resources. Common sense should tell you that these employees are the ones who can help you the most. Most answers are found on the shop floor. This is why it is so important when rolling out any type of initiative that it is built on the positive things taking place. One should build on the pride and expertise of the workforce.

You will notice that our assessment tool includes a cohesive and consistent equipment numbering system. This is important to the development of equipment strategy and work identification. The next areas are work control and the computerized maintenance management system (CMMS). It does not matter if you have the best vibration group or preventive maintenance routes if you cannot execute the work on time. Many employees want to jump ahead and implement these sexy programs forgetting that the real key is "blocking and tackling." If you cannot do this well, all the other money spent is wasted.

Another misconception is that a new CMMS will solve all your problems. The CMMS is only a tool and is as good as you make it. Studies show that planning and scheduling will only give you a small percentage of improvement. *The real key is defect elimination.* The best way to achieve this is by developing an accurate equipment history and understanding where the potential problems exist. Many forget to set up their CMMS processes to give them this information.

The CMMS is only as good as the information in it. The real key is in getting control of the work. When you can get all work requests to come though the CMMS, you automatically slow down the reactive work.

Next, you must have clear priorities. All things cannot have an emergency priority. With proper definition, work priority and a ridged and strictly adhered to process, you can reduce the percentage of reactivity.

If you can get employees to start thinking of breaking the schedule tomorrow verses today, you will increase the work getting done. Second, if you get employees to think ahead to next week when it can be properly planned as well, that is even better. We believe that there is at least a 5% improvement on wrench time by doing just this if the current practices are extremely reactive.

The reason we spend so much time on these basic parts of the assessment is to point out that there are things that do not take much time to implement, but can give your company some quick wins. When doing the assessment, it is best to start by interviewing the supervisors. Get an understanding of their thoughts on barriers, and also reaffirm to them that this is not to say they are doing a poor job, but there may be ways to help them do better.

Front-line supervisors always have the hardest jobs. They tend to come from the shop floor. They may or may not have post-secondary schooling. They still go out on weekends with their friends from the crew, yet we expect a whole lot from them. They catch heck from both ends. They have a small amount of authority, whether real or perceived. Now we are going to ask them to change and become more like coaches and mentors. They often feel that they may even be blamed or replaced. That is why you need to help them understand what is happening and how this will benefit them and their crews. If you can win over the supervisors, it will be much easier to also win the crew. *Sample interview questions are included at the end of this chapter.*

When you have completed interviewing the front-line supervisors, it is time to talk with the crews. This should be done either on a one-on-one basis or in very small groups, as employees tend to not speak up in large groups. We like to do the interviews first and then focus on getting the data from the CMMS, accounting, or the human-machine interface (HMI) systems. The interviews tend to lead you to find additional helpful information.

Now that you have let people know that their opinions matter, we recommend doing "Day in the Life" or DILO studies. This is when you observe with the operator or mechanic what is taking place in their world. This allows you to personally observe the barriers and problems they are facing. Most people are happy to show you where the problems are, especially if they know it is your job to help improve things. Never use names when reporting findings. Do DILOs with both operations and maintenance employees. Make sure to observe supervisors also. *Sample DILOs are included at the end of this chapter.*

When the interviews and DILOs are completed and the data is collected, you can start using the assessment tool in a small group setting. We recommend a cross-functional team of employees from all different parts of the facility. This group should be limited to eight employees or fewer. Six would be ideal.

When conducting the assessment, you should put great emphasis on the fact that items mentioned cannot be just "kind of" or "sort of" in place. If you give credit to anything that is just half way working, it tends to give the impression that it is more than it is. Also, point out that this will allow some quick wins and show improvement.

As stated earlier, it is important for employees to see and believe that there are some victories out there within reach. Victory produces more victories, as employees naturally want to be winners. Temper your toughness with consideration as well, so as not to be seen as inflexible.

Now that you have the results you need, it's time to get back to upper management and the steering team to obtain their buy-in, as well as their input. *The real goal is to let everyone have some say or input into this project.* Then you have a group of owners to support it. There are many ways to achieve operational excellence, but to get the speed and sustainability needed, you must allow some flexibility in direction. Dealing with employees is non-linear change. Do not concede on the important issues, but be smart enough to know the ones that are not. Now, you can start the implementation planning.

Developing an Implementation Plan

Now that the assessment is complete, you can develop the implementation plan tied to the business case. You have seen how to align the goals in an organization. You understand how to manage and lead from Chapter 9. Developing the implementation plan helps put a lot of this into practice. Here is a sample result of an assessment for our tool, 34% complete:

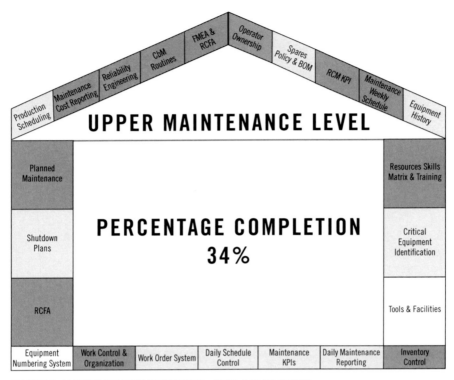

FIGURE 1: HOUSE OF MAINTENANCE – 34% COMPLETION

Dark Grey indicates not complete. White indicates completion (in this case, 34%)

As you can see, it is harder to start out with an assessment that looks like the one above than one that looks like Figure 2 on the opposite page, in most cases, 63% complete.

We have found that most manufacturing companies tend to have an equipment numbering system, but it is either not consistent or equipment is missing. The other rather common practice is "shut down management." Most companies do a better job at this than in

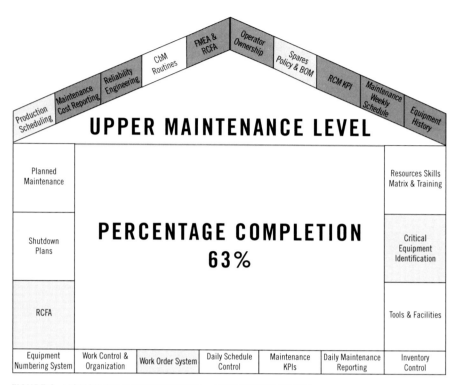

FIGURE 2: HOUSE OF MAINTENANCE – 63% COMPLETION

Dark Grey indicates not complete. White indicates completion (in this case, 63%)

normal running because most budgets are about 50% shut down work and 50% normal maintenance. You can notice that there is rarely a zero in any box. These functions always take place in some kind of format, but not to the standard of operational excellence. This means there is usually something to build on.

Now let's take for example the "Work Control and Organization" chart. If you look at the set of questions, it lays out the next steps. Here is the set of questions and the results for the first assessment:

No.	Work Control and Organization	Possible Points	Current Rating
1	The supervisory organization welcomes, solicits and listens to all levels of the organization. (1 point)	1	0
2	Maintenance supervisors have an adequate amount of time to control work. They spend:	3	
	(a) At least 80% of their time supervising their personnel in the field. (3 points)		
	(b) 70% to 79% (2 points)		
	(c) 50% to 69% (1 point)		
	(d) Below 50% (0 points)		0
3	Supervisory roles and responsibilities are clear and remain so within participative management concepts. (0-2 points)	2	0
4	Mechanics are at the job site working within fifteen minutes of the start of the shift and do not quit for cleanup sooner than fifteen minutes before the end of the shift. The following percentage of workday is lost due to these factors:	2	
	(a) Less than 3% (2 points)		
	(b) 4% to 5% (1 point)		0
	(c) Over 5% (0 points)		
5	Maintenance supervisors assign and control manpower in a way that assures good productivity — ensuring that jobs start on time, are performed according to quality, craftsman like standards with proper cleanup, and are completed on time with crew transition to their next assignment. (1 point)	1	0
6	The supervisor checks the quality and completeness of jobs:	3	
	(a) 90% to 100 % of the time (3 points)		
	(b) 70% to 89% of the time (2 points)		
	(c) 50% to 69% of the time (1 point)		1
	(d) Below 50% (0 points)		
	Work Control and Organization Possible Points	12	
	Work Control and Organization Points Awarded		1
	Current state of effectiveness awarded over possible		8%
	Points Possible minus Points Awarded		11

This tells you that the implementation plan should focus on supervisory training. There should be an emphasis on time management, coaching, setting expectations, goals, and roles and responsibilities. Of course, this has to be done in conjunction with other boxes in the assessment, such as daily schedule control and setting priorities. We like to begin with the foundational steps and have them more firmly in place before working on the higher level boxes. It does not mean that if you see opportunities in upper boxes that you should not take advantage of them, rather the focus should be on getting the "blocking and tackling" or basics done first.

Timing of these activities depends on many things. The size of the organization is a factor. Is this a pilot or the whole plant? The number of employees set aside for the implementation team, the amount of time employees can be pulled out to be trained, and the sense of urgency behind the needed changes are all factors. On average, the amount of time to get these changes through takes at least a year for the foundational piece and closer to two years for the upper ones.

There was a time when we would try to do all these pieces in six months to a year. We found that when we went too fast to get all the personnel trained, we lost understanding. It became something that was force-fed and not enjoyed. Also, the real benefits take some time to become apparent, so the value was misunderstood. The other problem was that once the implementation team went back to their normal jobs and the pus was gone, employees slowly went back to what they knew and were comfortable with. That is why we recommend having "aggressive patience" and getting employees to see the value first before biting off too much.

Here is a sample list of activities in an implementation plan. They are broken down by category and area. Each of these items should be set up and put in the time line. The assessment tool drives most of this, and practical knowledge the rest.

Teams
► Area teams
► Orientation meetings
► Maintenance
► Production
► Shipping
► Trucking
► Reliability teams
► Training
► Effective meeting training
► FMEA/root cause
► Problem solving
► Maintenance excellence

Review Current Processes
► Management control and reporting
► Improve shutdown planning
► Validate assessment results
► Review downtime log
► Improve management reporting
► Review root cause meeting
► Review roles and responsibilities in all areas

FMEA RCM Simplified Training

- Review critical equipment analysis
- Conduct FMEA/root cause training (all employees)
- Monitor for progress

Inventory System

- Critical spares identification
- BOM development
- Spares min/max improvement
- Tool room improvement

Preventive Maintenance Routines

- Review PM completely
- Review lubrication
- Conduct further FMEA
- Monitor for effectiveness
- Improve check sheets and training
- System for nameplate data collection

Production

- Daily, weekly operating report
- Develop control systems
- Review OEE
- Review KPIs
- Review downtime reporting
- Review SPC charts
- Review production startup meeting
- Incorporate safety and environmental meetings
- Review daily maintenance meeting
- Daily schedule controls
- Job descriptions
- Develop a bi-weekly production plan

Maintenance Best Practices (assessment tool)

- Identify present status
- Implement system for progression
- Review success

Training

- Skills training
- Personnel training/management training (assessment)
- Production conference
- Planner scheduler training
- Reliability engineering training
- Performance training
- Leadership training
- Employee development
- Communication skills
- Implement training
- CMMS training
- Conducting effective meetings

You will notice that if it says review, it assumes they are in place. If it says develop, then you are starting from scratch. Also, after most areas, there is time given for monitoring performance. This is where we spoke about not going too fast. If this step is left out, it will be hard to sustain the improvements.

Defining the Resources and Steering Team

We wrote about the steering team in Chapter 1. This is the high powered executive group that is sponsoring the project and also giving the top down support. This group normally consists of either the CEO or a senior vice president and general managers of related areas of focus. Their involvement ensures that the appropriate support is present, and when there are questions of direction, they are the sounding board as well.

One of the best ways to use this team is to have employees who work on the shop floor involved. In many cases, this may be the only time shop floor employees meet and discuss issues with employees of this caliber. It is always a win-win when employees can share their excitement about the new processes with the steering team.

When defining full-time, dedicated operational excellence team members, our rule of thumb is one person for every 150 employees affected. So if you have a facility of eight hundred personnel, we would recommend a full-time team of five to six employees set aside from their primary function for the duration of the implementation. In today's lean economic climate, this may seem unattainable. This is when you need to look at the depth of experience and number of employees you have. At this point, you may need consultants or some form of temporary help, such as retirees or temps.

This book is written for the knowledgeable to have a basic guideline and set of tools to achieve operational excellence in-house. You must look deep within the organization to decide if you have the time, employees and ability to take this on. We truly believe that sometimes it is better to get an outside view. Someone not steeped in tribal lore can give a different perspective to the team. This can be invaluable. We will discuss this in detail further in this chapter in "When To Use Consultants." One thing to consider is hiring one consultant at least to help set things up and come back periodically to see that things are still on course. If you can pull the rest off with your own employees, you will then have better trained, more competent, built-in sustainability leaders after the implementation is complete. Not to mention, you will have saved a pile of money.

Once the operational excellence core team is set, we segment the facility in areas and process teams. If the plant is managed in an area-based system, we recommend having two employees from each area designated as operational excellence representatives. Their time commitment should not be such that they cannot do their primary function with only minor disruption. They need to be given enough time so they fully understand the change process and can communicate to the shop floor what process changes are occurring and how they will affect the area. They also are used as subject matter experts in laying out changes to help make them realistic and functional. This is also the best way to get buy-in and a degree of ownership that is needed for sustainability. It is best if the team can consist of a front-line supervisor and an operator or mechanic. They should be employees who are respected in the area. This lends a great amount of credibility to the project when they are on board.

The training for these teams should consist of best practices in training, working in teams, dealing with adults and holding effective meetings, as described previously in this handbook. This type of training can be done in less then a week, and requires taking your team out of the workforce temporarily. We recommend one day sessions with at least a day in between. This allows the team to think about what they learned and talk to employees. At this pace, it is not such a strain on the operation and the team will not feel pushed. It may take longer, but shop floor employees are not used to long training sessions. However, when you do schedule your training, make sure the training is not interrupted and the team can give their full attention to it.

When to Use Consultants

There is most definitely a place for consultants in the pursuit of operational excellence. It is always easier to see the operational practices if you are not doing them. In other words, your view in the dogsled team is limited to what is in front of you. The lead dog may see what is ahead, but not what everyone else is doing. That is why it is important to have someone with the practical knowledge of operational excellence who is not caught up in the "dog team" of daily operations.

Some companies opt to find this expertise internally, while others look to consulting firms. There is no right or wrong answer. We recommend you do your homework well by visiting facilities or at least talking to others who have used the consultants. Be very focused on true results and partnerships. Make sure that their methodology fits with yours. Check to see that it was a joint effort and everyone had a stake in the success of the project. Was there a real sense of teamwork with the consultants? Once more, we tend to ask the shop floor as well as the management team.

When selecting a consulting firm, make sure that the employees you meet and talk with will be the ones doing the work. Many consulting firms do what is called a "bait and switch." During the initial assessment and start up, you meet their best employees, but when the work starts, most, if not all of the consulting team is replaced with less senior people. Make sure you get the consultants that best fit your facility. We believe in a staged, slower approach. But if you decide to do a fast track with many facets, having this kind of help is invaluable. Consultants tend to lend more credibility, not only to the board and senior management, but also to members of the shop floor, if they are properly chosen. They also can help you stay more focused. We also believe that there must be clearly stated deliverables and timelines in the contract. If the consultants have no "skin in the game," they are less likely to drive the results you may want.

Why a Pilot Project?

Depending on the size or number of your facilities, you may want to do a pilot project. We highly recommend this, as all change is non-linear. This means you learn as you go in some cases, and with a pilot project, you get better with each progression. We have seen instances in which the plant is divided into areas and one area is chosen for the pilot, or a mid-size facility in a large corporation is chosen. Once again, it depends on the situation and timing. Once a pilot is completed, you may want to do two or three plants or the rest of a large facility. Implementing a pilot allows time for the handbook to be understood and for a road map to be completed. Having a guide like this will be immensely helpful. You need to break out every important aspect and compile them into handbook format so future generations have a guide.

Presentations, Roll Outs and Tools

Two of the most overlooked parts of implementation are developing the right presentations and excellent presentation skills. It is always best to go with simple and direct bullet points and clear readable charts and graphs. Most people try to get as much as possible on a slide, but it confuses the audience and people lose focus. Also, as we have said previously, the people doing the presenting should be the facility personnel. They have their best impact when speaking from what they have experienced and not from a pre-programmed set of PowerPoint slides.

Every time you present, especially in the beginning of the implementation, you need to review the purpose of the presentation or the "why are we doing this" statement. This should be clearly and simply worded. Show the business case. It is said you need to be dipped seven times before it sinks in. We have always felt it is more like seven times seven. Once people understand that it is important and the reasoning is sound, let them know it is supported from the top and not just a flavor of the month. This reaffirms that it is a long-term commitment to change the way things are done.

When conducting the roll out, be sure the CEO or the senior executive sponsor is at every meeting. Leave no one out. It is important to let people know that operational excellence will touch everyone in the facility, even the CEO. Once things get going, do not stop having meetings with the plant personnel. Quarterly updates are not a bad thing. Keeping the momentum will be tough, but letting people see the commitment is key.

As you start to see improvements, celebrate. Do not wait for a year to show progress. Celebrate just having something changed, such as being able to schedule work better. Many companies not only have low hanging fruit, but fruit rotting on the ground. Grab what you can and buy-in will follow.

Once people get used to the idea that change is happening, they are more open to further change. Operational excellence looks at the facility from a holistic point of view. Processes and systems, as well as the organization, are all affected. Change is best accomplished with ongoing training doled out in segments. Once you start, do not stop until you are at the place you want to be. Slow change is slow death, but continual change is unsettling. What you want is for people to be looking for the next one percent to two percent improvement now that you have set things in place. After time, the fruit will be higher in the tree, but you want people to be focused on getting it. Continuous improvement comes from people being open enough to constantly reexamining themselves. Find the gaps and drive forward. It is important to have people in place whose job it is to drive necessary changes. To sustain all the good improvements will be difficult if there is not constant review. We have found that when there is someone in the organization whose job is sustaining continuous improvement, the chances of long-term success greatly increase.

The operational excellence manager, for lack of a better term, needs to be a special kind of person who is willing to be open to the organization's needs. We recommend that you bring in outside help, such as the consultants you may have used to do annual assessments. Sometimes, it may be even better to bring in a different consulting group. They may see things that the other consultants didn't and give you a different perspective.

You need to develop a culture of dissatisfaction. In other words, develop a culture of constantly looking for the next improvement of 1% or 2%. Where failure is not acceptable and preventive maintenance is seen as key to success.

Interview Questions

1. Tell me about your job.

2. What do you know about operational excellence?

3. What are your goals for the year?

4. What good things are taking place here?

5. Do you see a need to improve?

6. If you where in charge, what changes would you make?

7. What is the biggest thing that keeps you from getting there?

8. What is the biggest plant problem you continually face?

9. How would you fix it?

10. Are jobs laid out clearly and completely for you?

11. What role do you think you play in the organization?

12. Do you have a set of roles and responsibilities to show me?

13. What key performance indicators have meaning to you?

The key is to let them tell you, not the other way around. Here you will find the most value-adding ideas if you are open!

A day in the life of Supervisors -DRAFT-		ABC co	A day in the life of a Planner -DRAFT-		ABC co
Hour	Task	comments	Hours	Task	Comments
5:45 - 6:00	Ascertained with the production foreman minute changes and events		6:00 - 6:15	Inspects incoming messages	
6:00 - 6:15	Sort Jobs		6:15 - 6:30		
6:15 - 6:30	Supervisor informs planner of changes		6:30 - 8:00	Supervisor informed planners about current events Planner creates new work orders	
6:30 - 7:30	Time tracking of employees from the previous day		8:00 - 9:00	Planning of future contracts including material disposition	
7:30 - 8:00	Assignment materials and spare parts		9:00 - 9:30	Pause	
8:00 - 9:00	Support the work and information exchange on progress on the spot	Worked with corporate	9:30 - 12:30	Planner checks on material availability	
9:00 - 9:30	Pause		11:30 - 11:45	Agreement on scheduling for next day production with S&V	Ideally, confirmation of the plan from a week ago
9:30 - 10:11	Support the work and information exchange on progress on the spot		12:00 - 12:15	Agreement on scheduling for next day production with S&A	Ideally, confirmation of the plan from a week ago
10:11 - 10:42	Organization of a trouble-shooting	nice idea	12:30 - 12:45	Consultation with Supervisor for the next day	
10:42 - 12:30	Support the work and information exchange on progress on the spot	working more with the corporate support	12:15 - 12:45	Changes for tomorrow inputting	
11:00 - 11:30	Check priorities of the backlog of planning and production		12:45 - 13:30	Planning of future orders, care of the backlog	
12:30 - 12:45	Consultation with Supervisor for the next day		11:00 - 11:30 Thursday	Check priorities of the backlog with supervisor and production	
12:45 - 13:00	Inspection of all construction sites in order to exchange information on progress		11:00 - 11:30 Friday	Edit Plan next week	
13:45 - 14:00	Finish plan for tomorrow		13:30 - 13:45	Review plan for tomorrow	
			13:45 - 14:00	Takes part in passive layer transfer (only as a listener)	Plan is not discussed!

FIGURE 3: An Example of a "Day In the Life of" a supervisor (DILO).

1. Start working with your steering team to determine if you want to do a pilot area first or plant-wide implementation.

2. Define your implementation team and consultants, if you plan to use them.

3. Assess the gap based on your previous task of mapping the processes you want.

4. When interviewing, if you see quick wins, remember to take advantage of them.

5. Make sure that in all of the roll out meetings, the CEO or chief sponsor is there. Leave no one out.

6. Communicate, repeat, and communicate again.

7. Move at a pace that does not leave people behind or unduly disrupts the organization, but move fast enough so results are evident. Remember, slow change is slow death. Once you start, keep going.

●●● ⊘ COMMITMENT CHECK 15

❶ Once you start out, there is no turning back. Everyone will be watching your actions and deeds to see your true commitment.

❷ As the sponsor or even team member, you have to confront your team members if they do not live up to the expectation of "walking the talk."

❸ This is non-linear change. Remember to be flexible if one of the paths or processes needs to be altered or changed. Take ownership in the results, not the systems or processes, as they will change.

If you have completed the study of this handbook and followed the instructions in the "What To Do Next" sections, you are well on your way to operational excellence. You are having many successes and are beginning to realize the benefits of your work. However, you have also encountered some resistance from most levels of your organization. As you know, that is normal and natural and you kept going. The pages that follow share some of the thoughts and situations faced by others who undertook change efforts.

Please read them carefully to confirm that others have encountered many of the reactions that you have. They kept going and so have you! Congratulations!

... and that is our best advice.

*"Every moment is a golden one
for the one who has the vision
to recognize it as such."
— Chinese Proverb*

Making Change Stick   16

"Change is good for everyone as long as I don't have to change. The world is crazy and I'm the only sane person." This is the typical way people think. Resistance to change is as inevitable as death and taxes. It is also the biggest reason operational excellence often fails to be sustained. It is hard for change agents to come to terms sometimes with employees' thinking. "Why don't they get it?" is often what we hear.

It is easier if you have compelling reasons for change, such as, "If we don't get our costs down, we could all be out of work," or, "Our work will be more satisfying and this will be a better place to work." When employees understand the true purposes of operational excellence, it allows you to move faster and it has a better chance of being sustained. Of course, if they have heard that first reason for years and their company hasn't shut down, they may think it is just another snow job. Another typical reaction is, "This is our new implementation for the year." In other words, they start something every year and this is just the flavor of the month. This thinking is very common in larger organizations. We have actually met people whose job it was to just handle all the new things coming out of corporate.

One person told us that operational excellence is like trying to push a chain up a hill. So why do we do it? We do it because it really does works. Throughout this handbook, we have given you tips and guidelines so you won't get tripped up. It is important to be aware of hearing the unspoken word. It is not the person who is airing a distrust of operational excellence in a meeting that you have to worry about.

It is the person in the back of the room who says nothing at all. As the leader of change, it is your job to get people to talk and be involved. It may seem like a little thing to you, but it is not a little thing to them. There are so many little changes you can make in the organization that are the "quick wins." They may, in the overall scheme of operational excellence, not be very important but it will show people that they are important. *Sustainability is about the little things.*

A little more about change: research psychologists tell us that by the time a child is nine years old, 80% of what the child will believe and be for the rest of a typical, normal life is in place1. It is incredibly difficult to change a person. That's why careful parenting is so important. Who is training and implanting the ideas, culture, work habits, understanding of right and wrong, and human skills in these young people? You know the answers.

Later on, these young people come into the workforce. Some are prepared for the challenges of today's fast-paced, computerized work, and some are not. Your enterprise has received and will continue to receive a cross-section of young and older people who may seem to be the same, but in many cases, they are very different. You will have a difficult time sustaining operational excellence unless you find a satisfactory way to indoctrinate and train these newly arrived resources.

Our experience tells us that the first supervisor the new employee has when arriving at a new job is the most important person that employee will encounter while he or she is employed by the enterprise. This is where your culture, general expectations and your adoption of organizational excellence must be carefully explained. But more importantly, these new people must see it in action. Be sure to choose your best supervisors for indoctrinating and training new people.

Let us remind you at this point that there are no new people. We are all used and in many cases, abused. Remember that these people became about 80% of who they are and acquired what they believe by age nine. They continued to be educated in many formal and informal ways (in school and on the street) by who knows whom. Now you have them, and you have the task of fitting them into your culture. This is an awesome responsibility. Unless it is done well, these employees can bring ideas and habits that will be detrimental to the sustainability of your operational excellence project. Of course, you want their creativity and helpful ideas, but you don't want behavior and ideas that are counterproductive to continuing with operational excellence.

It is a good idea to write an employee handbook that describes operational excellence and make it required reading for all employees. Then, hold periodic meetings to discuss the handbook and get feedback on problems and successes. All employees, at *all levels*, must be committed to the purposes and processes of operational excellence if it is to be sustained.

The companies that are able to sustain operational excellence have some very interesting things in common.

1. All new employees must go through thorough training about the company culture and its direction.

2. They are strict about the processes.

3. They hold people accountable to the processes, but also hold them accountable to improve them.

4. Each year, successful companies routinely assess themselves and openly point out shortcomings and then develop new goals and actions to improve. (This goes back to the rigid process mapping and goal setting systems that you learned about in Chapter 7 and Chapter 8.)

5. Process maps are updated on an ongoing basis.

6. Successful succession planning. In well-run facilities, turnover is usually low. People have a life and their work is enjoyable and allows for creativity. They develop their people, and when change does happen, the next person steps in and the culture just continues to grow.

When companies change people, especially managers, often it is almost impossible to sustain organizational changes. It actually requires a consistent effort of four to five years for operational excellence to become embedded into the organization. *Staying with it is the true test of commitment.*

Continue to do what you have learned from this handbook. Always look for new opportunities to improve what you do and operational excellence will truly become a way of life and produce the benefits we have described for you. We wish you the best!

Your authors,
Dr. Bill Boothe and Steve Lindborg

For questions or to contact the authors email: mrostore@mro-zone.com.

About Reliabilityweb.com

Created in 1999, Reliabilityweb.com provides educational information and peer-to-peer networking opportunities that enable safe and effective maintenance reliability and asset management for organizations around the world.

Activities include:

Reliabilityweb.com (www.reliabilityweb.com) includes educational articles, tips, video presentations, an industry event calendar and industry news. Updates are available through free email subscriptions and RSS feeds. **Confiabilidad.net** is a mirror site that is available in Spanish at www.confiabilidad.net

Uptime Magazine (www.uptimemagazine.com) is a bi-monthly magazine launched in 2005 that is highly prized by the maintenance reliability and asset management community. Editions are obtainable in print, online, digital, Kindle and through the iPad/iPhone app.

Reliability Performance Institute Conferences and Training Events (www.maintenanceconference.com) offer events that range from unique, focused-training workshops and seminars to small focused conferences to large industry-wide events, including the International Maintenance Conference, now in its 26th year.

MRO-Zone Bookstore (www.mro-zone.com) is an online bookstore offering a maintenance reliability and asset management focused library of books, DVDs and CDs published by Reliabilityweb.com and other leading publishers, such as Industrial Press, McGraw-Hill, CRC Press and more.

Association for Maintenance Professionals (www.maintenance.org) is a member organization and online community that encourages professional development and certification and supports information exchange and learning with 10,000+ members worldwide.

A Word About Social Good

Reliabilityweb.com is mission driven to deliver value and social good to the maintenance reliability and asset management communities. *Doing good work and making profit is not inconsistent*, and as a result of Reliabilityweb.com's mission-driven focus, financial stability and success has been the outcome. Over the past 12 years, Reliabilityweb.com's positive contributions and commitment to the maintenance reliability and asset management communities are unmatched.

Other causes Reliabilityweb.com has financially contributed to include industry associations, such as SMRP, AFE, STLE, ASME and ASTM, and community charities, including the Salvation Army, American Red Cross, Wounded Warrior Project, Paralyzed Veterans of America and the Autism Society of America. In addition, we are proud supporters of our U.S. Troops and first responders who protect our freedoms and way of life. That is only possible by being a for-profit company that pays taxes.

I hope you will get involved with and explore the many resources that are available to you through the Reliabilityweb.com network.

Warmest regards,
Terrence O'Hanlon
CEO, Reliabilityweb.com